Peas are Gross

and other important insights about life

Carlee J. Hansen

Tina,

Thanks so much for liking the page! I hope you enjoy the book... Be sure to eat your veggies!

— Carlee Hansen

Printed by CreateSpace, an Amazon.com Company

Library of Congress Cataloging-in-Publication Data

Hansen, Carlee J, 1982-
Peas are Gross and other important insights about life.
ISBN-13: 978-1502751645

To my babies. Know three things:

If you put your mind to it, you can accomplish anything.

Humor exists everywhere. Find it.

I'll forever be your biggest fan.

Contents

Introduction

This is generally the part of the book where I qualify myself and help you to understand why you bought this fantastic piece of work. I'm supposed to throw out all sorts of important statistics about the degrees that I've earned, my successes as a professional business woman and the hardships that I endured as a teenager in the poverty-ridden streets of Davis County, Utah that encouraged me to press forward and find my inner hero. Well, let's start with a heaping cup of disappointment because I'm not going to do that. We are already off on the right foot; if we can begin with disappointment, we won't have much distance to fall, right?

You know that infamous line from our 37th President of the United States? Head slowly shaking: "I am not a crook." Well, now is the time for you to picture me with a Nixon mask on, offering up my own, slightly tweaked, rendition of that ever famous diatribe: "I am not an expert."

1

I'm an average girl with an extremely twisted sense of humor, a love for telling a good story and an uncanny knack for tracking down awkward moments in life and living them to their fullest. I figured that all of those things combined should produce an entertaining, if not totally uncomfortable, read.

So I decided to do what any aspiring reality star would do and try and make a buck off of living life. . . except with proper spelling and fewer fist pumps. (I'm not above fist pumps that increase popularity; I just realized it would be much more difficult to find a publisher for a book that required pop-ups and potentially, a built-in speaker). So here we are.

Wait . . . what? You just got a copy of a book that isn't written by a licensed therapist, dietician or marketing mogul? Why should you even read this garbage? Well I'll tell you . . . because I think it's funny. . . . And just in case you are worried about my previously mentioned awkward sense of humor and how you and I will get along, some other people think so too. Thanks, mom and dad.

This isn't a lecture. We get plenty of those about eating vegetables, keeping our living space tidy and managing our money. No, this is definitely not a lecture. Let's call it an attempt to call a spade a spade: this is how we live. And I hope you can find something in these pages to relate to but were too nervous to talk about before . . . or at least laugh at.

I've come up with a smattering of topics that I'd like to address, hopefully with a little humor. If this book *seems* disorganized and slightly random, it's because it is. You try and get this brain of mine to stay on one track for any extended period of time and then we'll chat. In fact, the order makes perfect sense to me because it's the order in which I thought about these things. Seems logical enough? Good.

I hope that you enjoy this read because I sure had fun writing it. If nothing else, I think it will prove that when we meet on the street (a well-lit one with plenty of people on it – I don't do dark alleys or strangers), you can rest assured that we'll have something to talk about.

Food

"I won't be impressed with technology until I can download food." –Unknown

If I had a motto tattooed on my forehead, there is an 85% chance that it would say "I'm only here for the food." That's embarrassing to admit but seriously, haven't we conditioned ourselves to make it all about the scrumptious morsels?

"What? You got a promotion? Let's go to dinner!"

"What? Someone died? Let's have a luncheon."

"What? You graduated third grade? Cake it is."

Seriously. From someone having minor surgery to getting their daily mail, there always seems to be an occasion to eat. I once ate an entire pint of ice cream just because my favorite re-run of Full House was on.

I say we talk about food, shall we?

It's called the vending machine taunt and I hate it. It's not hard to explain because I'm sure at least 75% of the population has suffered its wrath; the other 25% of you are eating Paleo or Jenny Craig or something similar so I'm not sure why you're reading this chapter in the first place – you're only going to end up hungry. Anyway, I digress. . . Sometimes I just want a treat from the vending machine. And by 'sometimes', I mean like three times a week. You can call it gross and that's fine. But sometimes I get desperate and those Pop Tarts don't actually look that bad compared to the alternative. . . a gut-wrenching nothing (the cinnamon candy at the receptionist desk equates to the same thing, FYI: a big, fat nothing)! Thank heaven that all work vending machines have a steady supply of Pop Tarts . . . or do they?

See, that's the issue. I never know. In my mind I build up this processed-brown-sugar-and-cinnamon obsession only to get to the break room and find that the regular stream of Pop Tarts have been temporarily replaced with some other (and might I add NOT CLOSE) substitute like, I don't know, fruit snacks. Dear Vending Machine Guy: even though the package is roughly the same size, fruit snacks are not a suitable substitute for Pop Tarts! One is a baked good (sort of) for crying out loud! There is nothing even remotely "bready" about fruit snacks unless they are found on my floor after my kids eat dinner. What are you thinking?

The only other vending machine tragedy that is equally offensive to replacing a staple like Pop Tarts with something comprised of completely different ingredients is what I like to call Flavor Alternating. Once again, we go back to the Brown Sugar and Cinnamon scenario. While climbing the vicious flight of stairs to the break room, I see that blue Pop Tart package as I reach the summit. But what is this? It's not Brown Sugar Goodness - it's Strawberry! I could (at this point) settle for the fruit-filled pastry by telling myself that strawberries are healthy if, of course, it was the only flavor option, but no. There, immediately behind the Strawberry concoction, is my real craving - Brown Sugar and Cinnamon - followed by another Strawberry and another Brown Sugar . . . you get the point. It's taunting me and I don't appreciate it. I, again, have come to a crossroads. Do I want the Brown Sugar bad enough to buy a pack of Strawberry as well and save it for a later date? **Side note:** please keep in mind that this would require another trip down said stairs to try and dig out more nickels from my desk drawer since the first round nearly left my change drawer bone dry to start with. Desperate times, people. We're in a recession!

Do I make camp next to the vending machine and try to coerce the next patron to purchase the in-the-way Strawberry pastry? Let's be honest, they likely won't buy anything with me hovering there anyway because vending machine food is "gross" or "classless" or "packed with unnatural chemicals" or whatever. But I can certainly try to make it look tempting by bringing up a variety of topics like "Hey, did you see that new Pop Tart commercial? Pretty amazing!" or "Hey, did you know that (fill in their favorite celebrity here) eats strawberry-flavored goodies like every day?" or, my personal favorite, "I overheard your supervisor saying that if someone brought them strawberry Pop Tarts, they would basically be next in line for a raise." (That last one tends to be a pretty good motivator, oddly enough.)

Or do I settle for Strawberry now and pray that sheer vending machine odds, though they haunt me currently, will allow me access to the better part of Brown Sugar tomorrow since nobody eats this stuff anyway?

What to do?

The point is this, bad vending machine loader man:

First, don't replace the steadfast. If you come to re-fill and all of the (insert candy of choice) here are gone, it's probably because that's what people eat so don't replace it with fruit snacks; no, it's not the same. No. It's not. Stop buying the Bit-O-Crappy candy bars that still occupy a full row in the machine after a month and only buy the good stuff.

Second, don't alternate flavors. There are very distinct audiences for these types of food. Regular M&M people aren't the same as Peanut Butter who aren't the same as Pretzel. You can't ask them to cross over. You are messing with nature. It is far better that you just don't HAVE one option than alternate options in a line in the machine and taunt all of your buyers. That's just cruel.

The only time it is acceptable to violate either of these rules is if there is CLEARLY a better alternative. Food is really subjective so this is hard to prove. You may (in my book) only do some sort of vending machine replacement if you are replacing my snack-of-choice with a $5 bill or replacing it with a breakfast burrito that is fresh and warm. No exceptions.

I know most of you are thinking that I can put a stop to this charade by just not eating out of the vending machine or by bringing my own delicious snacks to my desk from home. You're probably right. But I'm also not likely to win 'rational lady of the year' anytime soon and I'm coping with both realities.

PS - if your husband or brother or nephew loads vending machines for a living, please don't send me a PDF on 'Vending Machine Loading Etiquette' and why they do what they do. I'm sure there are reasons; they are just impossible to explain to my taste buds.

Follow-Up: For those of you that are curious about what I ended up doing about the Pop Tarts . . . I did the only logical thing I could think of: I waited until everyone left for lunch and bought the Strawberry pastry; and then I shook that vending machine like a mad woman until the Brown Sugar and Cinnamon ones fell out onto the floor. You know what they call that in most states? Resourceful.

Eat this

On more than one occasion, I've purchased or been presented with books that tell Jane Q. Consumer the right choices to make at restaurants or when having to make food selections at all; you know the breakdown – "Be shocked, this is actually healthier than this other choice that you for sure thought was healthier. Salads are sneaky little buggers." I generally sit and read them, riveted by the calorie counts of unsuspecting foods that are being exposed for what they really are – waist-lining mongers! And then, when my lunch break is over and I've polished off my last cookie, I head back to my desk and try to get back to my job.

These lists are shocking and tons of work is put into how many calories are put into Caesar dressing. But sometimes I wonder if maybe we are making this eating thing too complex, like maybe common sense should take over a bit and direct our eating habits.

So, in an effort to contribute to diet books across America (I had to put that phrase "diet books" in here somewhere. I'll get better exposure if I can fool a few people into thinking this is a diet book.), I have come up with my own list of food comparisons, you know, to guide you through this challenging world of eating. So, I present to you (in no particular order) "Carlee's List of Food Items That are Better than Other Food Items." (I worked on that title for weeks).

Just as a quick **side note**: I omitted anything with bacon included in it from this list – that's just an unfair fight. Bacon is to food like Danny DeVito is to the game Apples to Apples – it just trumps everything. I could technically title the "Better Stuff" list below "Bacon" and be done with this entire conversation, but I'd like to at least illustrate my point. Let's do this:

Stuff	Better Stuff
Apples	Apples with Peanut Butter
Celery	Celery with Peanut Butter
Oreos	Oreos dipped in Peanut Butter
Waffles	Waffles with Syrup and. . . .

(Can we just agree with where this peanut butter fiasco is headed and move on? But seriously – those last two. If you haven't ever gone there, it will change your life. Ok, moving on...)

Carrots, cooked or raw	No carrots, cooked or raw
Wet bread	Bread that is in no way tainted with liquid
Hot dogs made on the stove	Charred hot dogs made on the grill or over a campfire
Drinks shared with children	Drinks not shared with children that are floaty free

11

| Cinnamon-flavored candy | Anything that doesn't burn your tongue off |

Well, that about wraps it up. I really think that if you follow these simple guidelines, your food life will be much more enjoyable. And they said I couldn't write a book about proper diet.

Dating

"If I make you breakfast in bed, a simple 'thank you' is all I need. . . Not all this 'how did you get in my house?' business." -Unknown

Yeah, we're going there.

If there is one thing in this book that I like to think I'm a professional at, it's dating. No, not "professional" in the sense that I get paid for it, you sick-o. I'm not a prostitute. Although if I was, I'd like to think that I would be a classy one, for sure like Julia Roberts after she got rid of the wig.

I'm not a professional on this topic because I dated a lot either; my first real boyfriend didn't come until my 20s (wow, did I just say that out loud?) and 90% of my dates before that were with a good group of guys that were, unquestionably, in the friend zone – their words, not mine.

I did, however, have friends that dated a lot and I always seemed to be the sounding board (aka, the chubby friend with time on her hands to listen and observe) so I got pretty good at recognizing when things were going sour. I spent all of my teen years (plus a handful-ish) learning from other people's mistakes –and there were a lot of them.   I learned enough that I successfully dated and married a hunk of a man when I was 27 and he still isn't aware that he's been duped – how's that for skill? Not having much direct experience at dating, I had to make sure that paying attention would eventually pay off for me. Awkward girls – there IS hope but you have to pay attention!

Here is the great part: because you are reading my book, I'm going to tell you what I learned, kind of like a cheat-sheet for life. You can agree with it or not (I don't really care as long as you aren't reading a pirated copy of this and paid retail) but it hasn't failed me yet.

The Rules

Because we are so different, I'm first going to address the ladies. Sad to say it, we need the most help. Buckle up girls, reality is about to set in.

<u>For the Ladies</u>

Insight #1: Dudes like mystery, both in the movie sense and in real life. They like discovering and figuring out things for themselves. If your goal on a first date is to tell your fella everything about yourself so that at the end of the night you can make the claim that you "Really felt a connection" because you "talked for hours" and he even

14

knows "the name of my third grade teacher's cat", you are playing the wrong game.

Advice: Don't divulge everything at once. Too many ladies get this terrible disease that I like to call "diarrhea of the mouth" on their first date and talk about everything from their job to how it's their secret wish to have babies in a pool on their living room floor. (Do you know how many spell checks it took to even have the proper spelling of 'diarrhea' show up? That's a harder word than I ever gave it credit for.) These things scare dudes. Why? Because you talking about your birthing plan makes them think that he's the one that needs to memorize it; newsflash: he doesn't even remember your last name yet.

It will be an awesome surprise for your man if on the fourth or fifth date he finds out that you follow baseball. He'll think that you've got layers and he'll want to know more. Don't stifle him by telling him your hopes and dreams in the first 30 seconds – he'll think you are all surface (that's my nice way of saying "creepy") and that's no fun for anyone . . . except his friends that will hear about what a looney bird you are later. Dating pool: officially tainted.

Important **side note**: When you do divulge your inner beauty, be real about it. For instance, don't act like you love baseball if you don't. He'll figure you out when you tell him how the Baltimore Ravens are your favorite team and how Kobe is the best short stop in the game, hands down. Wrong. And then you'll be a fake – and ridiculous. Own what you like and he'll like you for it.

Second important **side note**: There is, in fact, a list of important things that you should NOT wait to divulge; things that you can't *casually* mention over a round of mini-golf. These are the exceptions to the above rule – the things that nobody wants to hear about four dates in. You'll need to take a look at your life to come up with your personalized list so when doing so, here is a good rule of thumb – if the statement you are about to make sounds ridiculous coming after "By the way. . ." you should probably get it out sooner than later.

I submit to you a short list of potential statements for sample purposes:

- "By the way. . . I have ten children."
- "By the way. . . I've been married nine times to four different men."
- "By the way. . . I'm really looking forward to the day that I can have sister wives."
- "By the way. . . I have a standing court date with possible prison time so I may need a rain check on that concert invite."
- "By the way . . . my therapist says that with continued work, I likely won't attack someone when they try to make physical contact with me."
- "By the way. . . I plan to return to my life on the nudist colony once I find a mate."

(See where I'm going here?)

Insight #2: Dudes like attractive women. Don't give me that "duh" look, I'm serious. You'd be surprised how many of us forget this little ditty and show up in public looking less than showered. Being attracted to their lady is important to them and if you try to ignore that because it's "shallow", you're out of luck. Believe me, I've tried to take the higher, altruistic, "he'll love me for my mind" road and it never panned out, not once. Important note: if you would consider yourself "homely" or "unattractive" or have ever been asked if you "live on a compound", keep reading; there is good news on the horizon. We'll get through this together.

Advice: Please note that there is a HUGE difference between attractive and hot (I shudder to even have this word in my book because I hate it so much in this context. What does that even mean? You glisten? You're sweaty? I don't even get it.). Guys don't require that you look like a model, strutting around with your hair just so and your makeup just so and your bum just so. They like those traits don't get me wrong, but they don't require them. (If they do happen to require them, move on. You'll be talking to yourself and/or your cat(s) after two years of marriage anyway).

Over the years I've noticed that the girls that are the best daters, the ones with the most interest from the fellas, aren't the "hot" ones; they are the attractive girls – the ones that take care of themselves (showering is a must); Be confident, smile a lot, be friendly, kind, smart and look put together. You'll notice that I didn't say anything about how their bums look. It was the attractive girls that had relationships and fell in love (insert favorite chick flick here – yeah, that's the kind of love I'm talkin' 'bout, yo!).

17

A little back story: I think I've made enough "chubby" references by this point for you to realize that I'm not a "hot" girl. I've been on the chubby side of the spectrum my entire life. For crying out loud one of my first topics of discussion in this book was food! So, since I seemingly couldn't control that part of my attractiveness (don't even get me started on diet and exercise – we'll get to that in a bit), I had to make a very conscious effort to make sure that the rest of my "attractive" ducks were in order if I was hoping to find my Prince Charming – I had to work on myself. (Work is hard – fair warning.) Here is what I did:

I went to school and watched ESPN and learned about random stuff so that I could carry on good conversation about a variety of topics. I learned more about "things" – baseball, cars and music, whatever I could learn even a little bit about. This made it very easy to start a conversation with anyone.

I traveled . . . a lot. Some of the best times of my life were traveling the world with my friends and it made me a better person – a little cultured and not so naïve. We went to Europe, traveled to concerts out-of-state, rented rooms in random hotels (whoa, whoa . . . again, mind out of the gutter) and got lost in sketchy parts of town. It gave me a sense of adventure and a confidence that I couldn't get any other way; if I could navigate Belize, I could get through just about anything.

Lastly - I showered. Seriously, I did. You might find this funny but think of "showering" as a basic reference to taking care of yourself physically.

I grew up playing sports and until I was in the eighth grade, thought that a sports bra was suitable underwear. . . and I was what they called an "early bloomer" so you can imagine the uni-boob issues that I still have to this day. Not great.

So, as I got older and wanted to engage the tougher gender (for purposes beyond a pick-up game in gym class), I knew I had to change. I bought nice(r) clothes, ones that were more flattering than a Spurs t-shirt but still comfortable; I resolved to only show up to a multi-gender event in basketball shorts if we were actually playing basketball or it was a car wash and I was the hired help. I wore dresses on occasion, even when there wasn't a funeral; I even did my hair – I had an amazing college roommate that taught me the power of the bobby-pin in turning an ordinary pony into a cute and trendy "messy" bun; I could have Prom hair like every day! I took care of myself in ways that showed that I was valuable – that I cared about me as much as someone else should. (I think that it also shows that while you may go through frumpy times in life, like say the first six weeks after you have a baby or like fifth through tenth grade like I did, there is always hope).

All of these things from learning to traveling and even taking care of myself made me more attractive; it didn't automatically shrink my waist size or give me the kind of legs that you only see in razor commercials, but it did change me. I gained more confidence as I learned who I was and what I wanted out of life. I still would say that I've never spent a day in my life being "hot" (other than those last two months of pregnancy and boy oh boy do I glisten with the best of them!), and I'm ok with that. But I will say that the work does eventually pay off and somebody (probably at least several somebodies in your case) will find you attractive. Then, you are in.

Insight #3: Dudes are like wolves. (Stop high-fiving each other, fellas. I'm not saying it like "They are animals on the prowl and we are their prey.") What I mean is that they don't like to be backed into a corner - aka being forced to make a choice between being taken over and attacking. In relationship language, we like to call these "ultimatums" and in real life, they don't work.

Advice: Ladies, this is the hardest lesson that I had to learn (translation – this is the hardest lesson that I had to watch countless friends learn while they were dating because remember, I didn't): you have to let your fellas make up their own mind in their own time. Please take note, this is not an excuse for him to be with you and not make any progress in your relationship for three years. This too, is unhealthy and super lame. I mean, if you haven't even changed your Facebook status by this point, there are some major issues.

What I am saying is that they need to be able to move forward in a relationship because they WANT to, not because they feel forced to.

There is a clip in one of my favorite British-turned-American comedy shows where the girl is desperate enough to keep her man around that she tells him that she is pregnant to keep him from breaking up with her. She's not pregnant of course and everyone watching laughs at how desperate she is to go to such lengths to keep her man. Silly girl with a complex. And then reality sets in and you find yourself awkward laughing at the clip because you realize that sometimes girls *can be* this crazy and actually do stuff like this all the time and you hope that you are never that desperate. Silly British comedy.

Over the years I've noticed that a lot of girls come to that point in their relationship where they make some derivative of the following statement: "We either need to get engaged or we need to end this". Don't look shocked, this happens all the time. You can replace "get engaged" with "move in together", "share a bank account", "have Thanksgiving with your family", "get large heart tattoos with each other's names" or a swirl of other terribly serious statements. Call it whatever you want, it all spells the same thing to the fellas: C-O-M-M-I-T-M-E-N-T.

I'm going to throw the boys a little bone here and say that they aren't afraid to commit, per se . . . . *when* they are ready. But if you back them into a corner and give them the ultimatum before they are ready, you will lose 100% of the time. Think about it, you are asking them to make up their mind between the status quo and a huge obligation in an instant and without all the facts. What will they choose? The easy way. No question. Here is why:

The parable of the new house

Let's say you are living at home with your parents (ah, the glory days of no rent and dinner on the table at 6:00). You are thinking about getting a place of your own – buying a house even. You've thought about it and looked up a few listings and even checked with a lender to see if you could get pre-approved. So, you call a real-estate agent and tell them what you are looking for – wood floors, a fireplace, a spa (yeah right, your first house? See why this is a dream?). Everything seems good.

The next morning, the real estate agent shows up at your mom's house (you don't have a place yet, remember) and says "I've found what you are looking for. It's a house with everything you want and it's in your price range."

You are ecstatic. You can't wait to go and see . . . wait. The real estate agent then says "Wait, don't you trust me? This is everything that you wanted. It's all on paper, right here. I'm afraid I can't let you go – you either need to sign this contract to buy the house right now or you have to stay living at your parent's house."

Seems like an abrupt end to the story, right? The agent seems totally unreasonable, right? Shouldn't you be able to make up your own mind and buy when you are ready? You didn't even get to see the yard! What if the roof is caving in? What if there are termites? So what if the house may technically have everything you want? What if it's secretly in shambles?

Nobody in their right mind would agree to sign that contract; they would take the easy, less risky way out of the situation and walk into the kitchen and ask mom "what's for dinner?" and settle in for a cozy night of "Murder She Wrote".

Ladies, I know that you are thinking "Yeah, but it's a house. It's a huge investment. I can't risk that and I had to choose one or the other, right there on the spot." Exactly. This is how the fellas feel when we make them make a decision before they are ready. Life with you is also a huge investment. They want to see you and what you are all about, they really do, but they won't sign the contract until they are ready and have seen what they need to; you have to give them the chance to check for "bugs", just like you wanted to check for termites. If you don't let them and you try to force it, it's over.

Please don't take this as saying that the dudes should have all the power and should get to decide when and where to move your relationship (seriously, guys you can stop high-fiving each other). Your relationship needs to progress and change or it'll never grow – you will never grow.

What I am saying is that the gents, the good ones, will make the choice when they don't see any other choice; and trust me, you want your fella to only choose you when they see no other option for themselves for the rest of their lives, not because of some ultimatum. That's when it lasts.

Ladies, I'm not a miracle worker. I'd like to say that following these rules will land you a man before that New

Year's party that you attend every year, but I can't promise that. I've known plenty of girls that have mastered the art of attractiveness and are still waiting on their prince – or even the friend of a distant cousin of a prince, but he still hasn't showed. Sometimes, they don't. You could go through all of this work and be the best you that you could be and it may take a while for a proper fella to show up on your doorstep. Why? Not because he's having issues with Google Maps. No, no. It's because we can't change nature and no matter how hard we work or how much we try, dudes can be dumb. But at least you'll have the most rocking version of yourself that you've ever known and there is nothing wrong with that.

This is where we transition into the dating advice for the dudes. Ladies, it's critical that you keep reading because if you mess up the stuff that I'm about to give you credit for, I'll hunt you down. I'll end up on the Today Show as the "Author that lost her marbles because the girls didn't listen" as opposed to "The charming new author that has made millions and we know why - we adore her too". Don't you dare ruin my chance to meet Matt Lauer under favorable circumstances. Don't you dare. I want the Today Show, people. Not Dateline.

For the Fellas

Insight #1: Dudes, girls aren't all crazy. I know that three of the last four girls that you took to dinner were pretty sure that you were destined to be together forever and that freaked you out – after all, it was one date and how "committal" can a bucket of chicken really be? I know that the heart-shaped note that one of them left on your car made your heart race faster than normal; not really the "In Love" kind of faster beat, more like the kind that that you hear in a horror flick when the guy realizes that the crazy chick killed his dog. And I know that you couldn't breathe when you came home and one of the other girls was in your mom's kitchen just chatting it up until you got home. "Look honey, she brought us all some cookies! Isn't she sweet?" says mom while you are secretly wondering if you should change the locks because she now knows the layout of your entire house. (Maybe, just maybe, I've seen too many Lifetime movies?) I know that I'm not helping my case by continuing on with these tall, albeit true, tales. My point is that I promise we aren't all crazy.

Advice: Please don't stop trying. I know many a fella who, once they come into contact with one of these girls that I like to refer to as "hyper-attached", run for the hills and basically drown themselves in a sea of microwave pizzas and the latest video game. I know that these girls can leave a horrible taste in your mouth like a bowl of black licorice and it makes it really hard to want to take out other girls when Hot Pockets (mmm. . . Hot Pockets) and WoW are just so much more comforting (and cheaper) than trying to impress the fairer sex.

When you come into contact with a "crazy", treat it like the CDC and control that sucker. Put on your hazmat suit, warn the public and get back out there. But don't assume we are all infected. I'm here to root for the good girls – the cool ones who really do just want to see where things go and are cool getting to know you – I promise they exist. Don't let Looney Linda turn you into a hermit.

The parable of the jelly beans.

I heard a parable from a friend once that makes my point. Since parables can be hard, I'm going to give you a cheat sheet just after this little story comes to a conclusion.

Dating is like a bowl of jelly beans. The first people to the bowl seem to pick and choose all of the great colors – the reds, the pinks, even the greens get snatched up until all that you have left is a bowl of black jelly beans. The black jelly beans don't get thrown away because, after all, they are still candy and one day, in a moment of sugar desperation, you may find yourself succumbing to the bowl and eating a black jelly bean; you will likely find yourself quickly spitting it out and rubbing your tongue with a paper towel, vowing never to eat jelly beans again, but you always come back to the bowl. Who knows, maybe someone will drop in a fresh bag with lots of colorful, delicious jelly beans and the black ones will no longer be the only choice. Probably not.

So that leaves us with two scenarios: first, your taste might change (not likely, but possible) and you may find that you don't actually detest the black jelly bean; the biggest issue here is going to be public perception – when all of your buddies are ragging on the black jelly bean, will you have the guts to eat it anyway? Man up, dude.

The more likely scenario (and the one that I vote for like it's a bill to decrease taxes) is that if you make your way through enough black jelly beans, you're going to get a surprise and find a dark purple; they always have a way of getting mistaken as something they are not, when really, they are some of the most delicious of the jelly beans – full of flavor and fruity and awesome without the gaudy appearance of the others. Somewhere in that bowl of black jelly beans is a hidden gem that has been left to harden because someone didn't bother to look close enough at the guts and see that it doesn't belong with the outcasts.

These purple beans, dudes, are yours for the taking. So TAKE THEM!

Parable Cheat Sheet:

Bowl of Beans: world of dating
Beans themselves: girls
Black beans: the girls that heart-attack your car after your first date and claim that "True Colors" is now your song because it was playing while you were ordering tacos.
Dark purple beans: the coolest chicks you will ever meet. These are the ladies that have mastered the attractive scale AND they aren't willing to flaunt it in front of your face. They aren't crazy, they are genuine. They are smart, they are fun and usually, not all the time but usually, they are cool enough to like or at least tolerate ESPN.
Other colors: obviously awesome girls, but easily noticed
Paper Towel: device used for cleaning . . . ok, maybe that one was obvious.

Insight #2: I actually think that if I keep referring you to the fact that not all girls are cray cray, you're going to be just fine. Oh wait, one more thing:

Insight #3: I know that women's lib likely happened before you were alive, which is why I am wondering why it still scares the pants off of most of you. I actually have serious doubts that most of you even know what women's lib was actually all about but you're continuing to use it as a politically correct excuse to be lazy and cheap - walking around like you are doing us ladies a favor by letting us get our own door and having us pay for our own club sandwich when we're out on the town. After all, we are the ones who wanted to be "equal", right?

Advice: Technically, it was our moms who fought that battle and we've (mostly) grown up in a world of equality across the board; we mastered Tonka trucks and Legos when we were small and even pretended to be Michelangelo while we played Teenage Mutant Ninja Turtles. So (and this is where it gets tricky) because we have felt so equal in everything else, we do, in fact, like to be treated like a girl when you take us out. Our moms were fighting for equality in the workplace and the right to vote, not for permission to be treated like barbarians and punched in the arm with a "good job" after a heated frame of bowling.

When you take a girly friend out for a night on the town, man up and crack open your wallet a little bit; hold doors and make plans because that's what real men do – they take control of the situation and act like gentlemen. Now

I'm not saying you have to lay your coat out over a puddle or anything (for goodness sake, if your lady can't even walk around a deep puddle, you are in for a real treat when you try to talk politics) but you can take polite control of the situation and show her that you've got your stuff together. There's a new generation of ladies out there boys, ones that watch shows with old English and a little thing called chivalry. The ladies may say they aren't doing this, but these girls are holding you to a whole new standard. So turn on some PBS and learn a few things, will ya?

Online Dating

If I had written about this even 10 years ago, there would have to be a sub-text on this section: "For nerds and hermits", because that was the perception of the online dating world at the time – only those who couldn't hack reality met on the computer. Not anymore, my friends. Online dating has become as normal as it gets. But why do they have to make it so darn hard?

Have you ever noticed that one of the first questions on your online dating profile is "body type"? While I know physical attraction is important (remember, we discussed "showering" and all that entails), would I even *be* online and unwilling to post a picture if I didn't have some sort of deep-rooted misgivings about myself? I mean, seriously. You do realize that almost everyone skips this question and comes back to it once they've convinced themselves that online dating is a judgment-free zone. Hahahaha, judgment-free. That's funny.

Just having to list your body type is daunting enough but having a drop-down of selections makes things way worse. I know it probably doesn't bother the fellas much because to some degree, you can take some pride in looking like a professional athlete but when the only 'body-type' selections are 'slim', 'normal' and 'looks like a fullback for the New England Patriots', a girl gets a complex. Here is the thought process:

'Well, uh. . . well I guess if I am being honest, uh. . . well, I mean I'm pretty normal but what does 'normal' mean? I mean I'm a little chubby but I've never been drafted by the NFL. Are there sizing charts on here somewhere? Can I type my own description? What if my version of 'normal' is different than a guy's version of normal? It is; I know it is. And then I become *that* girl – the liar. My online dating career will be over before it starts. He'll tell everyone that not only am I not "normal" but that I apparently can't read. But I've never even worn a helmet! Uh. . ."

This is especially troublesome when you have to make the chubbiest selection on the list because it's almost as if there is hidden text that only skinny people can see; people assume that because you are chubby, you also don't do your hair nor do you shower or shave on a regular basis – it's an odd correlation for me to accept, but it happens. If you choose the chubby selection, they should give you an option to explain yourself like "I'm chubby-ish but I wear nice clothes and have good hygiene. My dentist has my teeth on his website."

Can you smell the anxiety with all of this? I hate how the whole Q&A profile set-up works – asking you to not only select your body type from a drop-down menu but also to list all of your most important traits via checklist – "pick five adjectives from this list that describe you. . ." So, I should only have five? And what kind of an adjective is "superstitious" on a dating site? Does anyone actually choose that? "Hmm, well in addition to be honest and smart, I better let them know that I scare easily and believe in astrology. Yep, that ought to give me the matches I'm looking for. And . . . . submit."

I once wanted to look up the phone number for one of these services and talk to a representative about this very topic:

"Um, hello? Yes. I am trying to fill out my online dating profile on your site and I can't seem to find the appropriate adjectives that describe me. What do I want to add? Very funny. No, no – that's what I want to add: I'm very funny. No, I understand that 'funny' is on there, but I'm not that. I'm *very* funny. You see lots of girls list themselves as 'funny' because they laughed at a joke once but this is an important distinction for me – it's really all I've got, actually. Yes, I'd be willing to trade two adjectives for the price of one in order to list 'very' in front of 'funny'. Yes. I'll hold. . ."

I think what would really make these adjectives mean something is to have them be comparative in nature;

rather than listing "funny" it should say "funnier than. . ." and then you could tag people that you know in common to give the other side a point of reference. Here are some examples:

Are you more handsome than . . .? (Check all that apply)

- o Liam Neeson
- o Justin Timberlake
- o Our buddy Dave

This works on a lot of fronts – not only would it give you some scale to compare but you could immediately tell if someone is lying (you slip Justin in there and if it's ever checked, you know they either have a giant ego or are flat out cray cray. Trick question. Boom.)

For all the other kids. . .

My last piece of dating advice is really for the youngsters out there . . . or the parents who really need someone to have this talk with their teenagers because they aren't brave enough. Either way, I've got your back.

All of you old souls (you know, those of you who know what love is at a way younger age than everyone and you know that it's real, it really is, no matter what anyone says. . . they just don't understand), here is my thought for you: It's not real.

I believe in romance and I believe there are teenagers that are capable of understanding adult feelings, but I just believe that you can't understand true love until you have a high school diploma. (If you read the fine print, the diploma actually states that "You now have permission to fall in love with the person of your choosing." It's true – I can't make this stuff up.)

I know you are looking at your girl/boyfriend's picture while you are reading this and dreaming of the day when you will be together forever while simultaneously thinking "I wish my parents would get off my back and stop talking about curfew. Don't they understand what love is!?!?" Let me tell you why they won't lay off and it's the same reason I'm writing this in my book:

There has never been a love story that starts like this: "Junior High, romance, late dates, freshman year, prom night, pregnant" that doesn't end like this: "family fights, parent's basement, fast food shifts, food stamps, drop-out, single parent."

You aren't an exception, I promise.

Social Media

"Thank you for updating Facebook again with what you ate for dinner. The suspense was killing me."
-Unknown

After spending more than my fair share of time on the web (I mean, I've practically finished YouTube . . . twice), I continue to be amazed by what people are willing to post online for the masses to read. Seriously. No, no. . . . Seriously. Social Media is a mecca for comedic material. Cha ching!

Disclaimer: It's totally OK if you nervous-laugh your way through this chapter and innocently, yet casually look around and say "Psh, who would do that?" Just be sure to log-in and delete all the questionable stuff on your profile before this book becomes a best-seller. You don't want to be "one of them", do you?

The results of a bad status update or all-too-revealing blog can be far more catastrophic than drunk texting (at least in that instance, there are only a handful recipients of your late-night rant as opposed to your 600 closest friends, coworkers and in-laws). I think that as a failsafe, all social media outlets should have an "Are you sure?" pop-up that comes up before you are actually able to post something online. Just imagine the catastrophes that could help us avoid – if we had to read what we wrote twice. Maybe having an intervention on every post is too big of a nuisance? Maybe the pop-up could just look for trigger phrases that are potentially hazardous? I submit the following as a starting point for the trigger words: barf, boobs, drunk, itchy, mother-in-law, naked, poop.

The last several years have taught me a lot about life . . . and not just mine. I'd like to thank all of my FB buddies for teaching me all about your points of view on things. Here are a few things I've learned:

- Jesus doesn't support spam emails or photos on Facebook. In fact, He didn't even have Facebook when he was alive (that may shock some of you youngsters). Me not "liking or sharing" a picture doesn't mean I hate Jesus or puppies or my grandmother or you. It just means I don't want to. You're just silly for thinking any "are you worthy" questioning from the Big Guy in the afterlife has anything to do with photo sharing (unless it's of the naughty kind, of course. In that case, you've got some explaining to do.).
- Speaking of: All kids with odd diseases or unfair abnormalities are sweet and beautiful. I know that you think these photos need "likes" to prove it but they don't. They are adorable despite their circumstances. One hundred percent of people should agree with me and if they don't, they are heartless and don't matter anyway. And no, there

isn't a company or computer company mogul that is going to donate $1 to research said disease for every "like" their picture gets. No company is that unstructured . . . or that generous for that matter.

- Generally the people who talk the most about politics know the very least. These people are also the perpetuation of misrepresentation of political ideals (that's smartest sentence I've written in a while – thank you thesaurus). People who really know about politics are reading expensive magazines and papers on the topic, not arguing with their mates on social media. No, the news channel will not be calling you for your amazing insight about gun control or education reform or whatever your topic of choice is today, regardless of how earth-shattering your opinion may be. So leave your lipstick at home because you are not going live with GMA.

- On a related topic: You can find an article or info-graphic to support your thoughts on anything. That doesn't make it real or right or true. (But do feel free to use this book to support your ideals at any time . . . it's about as real and right and true as the news these days).

- Popping the world's largest zit is apparently more exciting than any other video on the internet. Are we embarrassed that this is the case? Even a little bit? This makes me want to throw up. Hey, maybe I can record my throwing up and. . . .

- eCards have made everyone funny. "Thanks funny people who write eCards for letting me post twisted Hallmark cards online and convince my friends that I'm funny too because I thought you were funny. My "likes" have gone up 30%."

It's amazing that six brief bullet points will give our posterity some insight into our psyche, right? A couple of other nuances that I've noticed that I think we had better address, you know, since we're already here:

I love . . . me!

What I love most about social media is that it's a total narcissist's dream; where else can you announce to your hundreds of friends how awesome you are and not look like a total jerk? (I know people that do this in person and they ARE jerks. . . I checked.) Can you imagine a face-to-face conversation that reads like a Facebook post?

"How's it going?"

"Oh my gosh, I have the best life! Seriously, it doesn't get better than this."

"Oh really? What's happening?"

"Well, I just made the best dinner (holds up a picture of spaghetti-stuffed bread) for the love of my life (holds up a heart) and the cutest kids that you will ever see (holds up an eCard that says "Hold this up if you have the best kids in the world"). I'm so amazed that I had time to do that after I did all of my laundry, painted my bathroom Chevron and got rid of that toe fungus I've been complaining about for weeks. Now I'm off to campaign for the "Mom of the Year" award for our mommies group at the zoo field trip today. Hashtag who is more awesome than me?"

If someone even tried to say something like that out loud, I'd need to high-five them . . . in the face . . . with a chair. I know a handful of you are very uncomfortable right now and wondering who would post something, let alone say something, that self-serving in one shot. But really, think about the social media updates you've read (I say "read" because I don't want to say "wrote" and have you stop reading my book). . . now put them all together in paragraph form. Sound familiar?

I hate my life . . . and yours . . . and Mondays.

I do suppose that being in a narcissistic nightmare is better than the alternative though: the Negative Nancy. I feel like I can't even log-in to social media without a box of tissues - it's the world's largest version of free therapy. Is this a status update or a country song?

I'm going to go ahead and play therapist (remember, no license here) and just solve all of the most commonly written-about issues for you right now. Let's do this:

Since the beginning of time, Mondays have been terrible. It's like during the creation, the Big Guy said "We're going to start with Monday and fair warning, it's going to be a rough one, people. You'll be tired and people will seem extra annoying. Worst of all? It's going to repeat, you guys. Over and over again." Unless Monday magically becomes lottery day or free candy day, I'm pretty sure this trend will continue. If we can all resolve to agree on that point, I think we can stop making the blanket "I hate Mondays" statement online. Deal?

The only thing that generally stinks as bad as Mondays is working. Regardless of how amazing your job is, I would bet on the fact that you'd rather be at the beach than working. So, when work is boring or hard or relentless, remember that 50 million other people feel exactly the same way (most of them are Tweeting about it simultaneously). As a **side note**, I qualify any and all of the following as "work": spreadsheets, emails (except the ones that have funny pictures of kittens or are from some prince in Nigeria wanting to share his inheritance, those are just good times), housework, yard work, or any other phrase that you can actually add the "work" suffix to and have it make sense. Consensus? No fun.

As a general rule of thumb, if you were to say your complaint out loud to someone's face and their only response would/could be "Oh," don't post it. That's life. We're all going through hurt arms and bad days and tired feet and broken lights. Crap happens.

Lastly (and this is critical), no matter what kind of funky disease or bruise or zit you have, nobody wants to see a picture of it.

Speaking of pictures. . .

The duck face? Are we over it? Can't we just go back to the good old days when the only pictures we had of ourselves either had a paint-splattered motif or were some sort of over-priced, awkward glamour shot in leathers or

40

stone-washed denim? At least in those instances there was no chance of me seeing a toilet in the background and I wasn't left wondering if you took the time to strike a pose before or after you finished your business.

Are you serious? Kidding? Serious?

More so than pictures, I just get so lost sometimes in what people are writing that I can't seem to make heads or tails of it. If I could turn back the clock, I'd re-take that college course on reading the sarcasm font. I'm terrible at it. Things have gotten progressively better for me since the introduction of the ever-helpful "LOL" and emoticons (Emoticon is not a dirty word. Google it; you use them. "Google it" is also not a dirty phrase, Mom), but I still struggle knowing when people are serious or not. See what I mean:

<u>Sarcasm Font</u>

"I am amazing."

"I hate my life."

<u>Literal Font</u>

"I am amazing."

"I hate my life."

Without a smiley face or an "LOL" after these statements, I'm just not sure if I should chuckle or if I should call 911.

Speaking of LOL . . .

There are a lot of things that people find funny that I just don't. At least I'm assuming they find it funny because it sure makes them laugh out loud . . . which is a pretty hearty laugh if you ask me. Maybe an occasional LIMH (Give it a second . . . here it comes . . . laugh in my head. You got it.) could be appropriate but certainly not an LOL. A few examples that confuse me:

"My foot just got ran over by a bus! LOL"

"My kid just drank Clorox. LOL"

"I just lost all of my money to a prince in Nigeria! LOLOLOL"

Did you really LOL when this happened? Is it really an NLOL – nervous laugh out loud – like secretly you didn't want to admit how dumb you are on the internet but you were forced into it at gunpoint? I hate when that happens. LOL.

"I'm in love, I'm in love, and I don't care who knows it." –Buddy the Elf

Beyond the exclamations of pain or reading through everyone's morning routine, by far my favorite social media interactions are the declarations of love. Some of the stuff that I read about relationships downright makes me blush; those seventeen-year-olds sure know what love is. Seriously, I'm surprised that major greeting card companies still exist after the sheer poetry that you can find on social media.

The most important thing of all time is the relationship status. We all know what it means to be Facebook "official" – it just got real, people (in the olden days, this may have been referred to as second base). This, however, can be a dangerous game if you aren't careful. Some pointers:

Never change your relationship status unless you've discussed it with the other party BEFORE updating your status; the words "together" or "boyfriend/girlfriend" should be mentioned face-to-face *at least* once prior to a status update. You don't want to be the creeper who goes from friends to "In a relationship" after one night at the movies, you weirdo.

Ladies, never be the first one to update your status – I learned this the hard way. In fact, it would be ideal if you and your significant other (after discussing it before, see pointer numero uno) could go all Mission Impossible and synch your watches and pre-determine a time to update your statuses and do it at the same time. I promise that if you don't, you'll be the loser that went first. You don't want that on your record, do you?

If the synching fails (like say you don't own a watch or you can't yet tell time), dudes, do us a favor and update first. For real. You never look like losers doing this – it's like you are marking your territory and claiming your woman. (Dogs do this by peeing all over an area; humans do it by updating their relationship status on Facebook. Please do not confuse these two tactics.) The girl will swoon and feel like you're her "man" and you will be that much cooler.

WARNING: Dudes, about the previous point . . . please make sure to always refer to the first piece of advice before proceeding with "being the man". If you feel like you are in a relationship with a girl because technically you sat three rows behind her one time and you knew she "felt a connection," you are wrong. Don't you watch 80s movies? She probably has some secret older boyfriend named Rocko that is going to come out of nowhere if you even attempt to talk to her, let alone claim you are in a relationship. Rocko was probably too cool to use social media and that's why she didn't update her relationship status earlier (because she couldn't tag him, of course) and you just assumed she was available so you claimed her and now you can't play ping pong because of that arm fracture. Thanks, Rocko. Thanks.

Lastly, and this is important for all of you youngsters out there. Strike that, this applies to everyone. Never use the "It's complicated" relationship status. What does that even mean? If you are below the age of 18, you don't even know what a complicated relationship is. He got transferred out of your gym class or can't take you to prom? Sob. Wait until there are kids and bills and things to worry about other than you, and then we can start discussing "complicated". You are either together or you're not, it's as simple as that.

Older folks, same rule applies. (You'll know you fall into this older category if you frequently use the word "folks".)

Using the "It's complicated" update is basically just telling the world, "I was in a relationship and am currently trying to salvage things. I am alone and bitter." Word to the wise, we all know that when you go from being "in a relationship" to "it's complicated", things suck for you and you should probably just cut bait. But thanks for the subtle insight into your crappy/creepy relationship.

Door is unlocked, key is under the mat.

The one and only thing that I'm hoping will never change about our social media usage is the need to announce where we are and how long we'll be gone . . . always. If this stays just as it is, I know for a fact that I will always have food on my table, if I choose to take up a life of crime that is.

Location, location, location. It's an old real-estate mantra that apparently the online community has taken to heart. If you are going to be at dinner for an hour and want to check in some place so that your friends know that you eat, good on ya, I guess. If you are planning to be gone for a week to a remote village with no cell phone access and you left your pearls (I know, it's a mystery novel cliché) on your nightstand, don't announce it. You might as well tell me where the key is so you won't have to pay for a broken window in addition to your now missing pearls. (Please note that when I say "me", I don't actually mean me. I'm not a thief. But that dude that you are "pretty sure" you know from high school that you just friended might be.)

I love seeing updates that say things like "Yes! Plane to Morocco leaves in 30 minutes. Sayonara suckers! I'm gone for three weeks!" because it tells me so much: first, you are going to be on a plane and un-contactable for more than a few hours. Second, you are going to be gone for an extended period of time. Lastly, if you are lame enough to post something like this, you likely haven't taken the time to see if your address and personal information are posted on the internet for all of us to refer to.

I'd appreciate it (as your unexpected house guest) if you would be so kind as to continue to post updates throughout your vacation so that I can know exactly when you will be home. I'll make sure to be packed up and out by then . . . oh and I'll let you know if you're out of milk.

I've said on several occasions that a great date night activity would be to spend an hour gathering a list of all of the people you know are out of town, look up their addresses on the trusty interwebs and go to their houses and leave a post-it note saying:

Knew you were gone. Lucky it was us and not someone shady.

Love,

The Facebook Bandits

Good times, right? That would scare them straight. Or at least I thought it would. The police didn't think it was as "constructive" as I did.

These location updates are most dangerous when paired with the next FB oversight:

You look familiar. . .

How do we know each other? If I can't (within 20 seconds . . . and that's stretching it) process how we know each other and recall the gleaming status of said relationship, you're not making the social media linking cut. Don't add people that you think you saw at the grocery store once to your friend list. It's not safe. You know that guy who you saw at that one sweet party that you talked to/asked to move his car so you could make curfew? He's not your friend. And he might be a creeper. (Please note that when I say "he", I totally mean "he" because generally, and the incarceration numbers can back me here, men are more of the PHYSICAL creepers. I will not, however, disregard the fact that you boys need to be equally as careful with adding the ladies so you don't end up with a bucket of crazy on your hands; she likely won't physically hurt you but she could *destroy* you otherwise).

Enough on this topic, I suppose. I've got some other business to attend to and some duck-face bathroom pictures to post (jokes, jokes. . . I take mine in the car) so I had better get to it. Happy Facebooking, all. And don't forget to share this chapter with your friends. . . I mean, only if you love puppies.

Exercise

"Whenever I say the word 'exercise', I wash my mouth out with chocolate." -Unknown

If only I could look cute in animal print work-out gear.

If you bought this book specifically for my chapter on exercise, hoping that I'd do a step-by-step breakdown of some new ab-buster workout, you, my friend, need to get your money back and re-engage Pinterest, the land of everything new and ground-breaking about exercise. (Did you see that one about shaping your bum and thighs? A-Mazing.) My version of "ab-busting" is eating so much that you literally think you broke something in your stomach. In fact, there is only a chapter on exercise because I figured it may index one day on Google and increase my sales.

No, no. The very length of this chapter should give you some insight into what you are about to read; This here will be a more cynical look at this thing called exercise and the extremes that we go to in order to show everyone else how healthy we are. That sounds like a more fun project than diagramming sit-ups, don't you think?

Important **side note**: Please know that my cynicism comes from a very real, honest place. I am truly this judgmental and would hate for you to think that I am just putting up this front for the sake of my book. I genuinely hate exercise and get angry at people that are good at it. You can call it jealousy, that's fine. Just know that this bitterness, it's sincere.

Let me kill all of your thoughts about this right now: I am not dictating this book into a recording device while I train for my next half marathon. I'm actually lying on my oversized couch in my pajamas, trying to ignore the alien in my stomach that is desperately calling out for a breakfast burrito. Tell me I don't have any will power. . . .

I believe in exercise – I really do. (I need healthy people to buy this book too . . . although with the growing obesity epidemic, it's much wiser economically for me to take the side of the chubbies like me and make fun of it at every turn). I think that we generally sit around too much and need to get up and get moving and get stuff done. Blah, blah, blah. That's all that exercise is really, right? It's moving your muscles and burning calories. And when you simplify it to this point, it really doesn't seem that bad.

I think where most of us get lost in the shuffle and get scared to exercise is that everything we see seems like we have to be extreme to accomplish any worthwhile progress: running isn't worth it unless you can go 26 miles in one shot. Yoga is only good if you are doing it in a room where the heat has been turned up to 105. Lifting weights is only effective when the weight is as large as a monster truck tire. This stuff intimidates me and frankly, makes me start looking for a donut.

While these extreme workouts are amazing for some people, they just aren't the right thing for everyone, despite what the infomercial tells you. I've done my fair share of running in my life but I usually do it with a purpose other than just to run; I played basketball and ran up and down the court. I played softball and rounded bases. I walked into sketchy dollar stores and needed to get back to my car without getting shot. But there was always a stopping point and it was never 26 miles away.

I remember the first time that I ran a 5k. I had trained and trained for months (I know you are snickering because a lot of people don't have to "train" to run three miles but you may as well have asked me to run 100) and by race day, the farthest I had run without stopping was two and a half miles. Needless to say, I was nervous about having to lengthen my previous 'best' by 30% . . . or die on the side of the road at some small-town fundraiser without an EMT on duty. I woke up on race day early and nervous, got dressed quickly and was still nervous, drove to the race nervous, waited around and was nervous and I ran nervous. But I ran. I walked exactly two times during the race for what seemed to be a long time but in all likelihood was probably about 100 yards and I finished the race about five minutes faster than I could have even predicted. . . because I was nervous (and had to pee. Talk about a motivator.).

When I crossed that finish line, I was prepared for this overwhelming exhilaration to hit me – I had accomplished my goal and couldn't be more proud! You can imagine my dismay when I crossed the finish line and the first thing that crossed my mind was "Well, that sucked." I had spent my whole morning (really, the whole previous two months) being so anxious about pushing my body beyond its current limits that I realized I hadn't enjoyed any of it – not the training, not the run itself, not even the finish. Why in the world did I do this?

Remember when yoga was starting to become all the rage? I felt all sorts of pressure to be a "yogi" and join the "in crowd" and essentially stretch for two hours a week until I could put my feet behind my head (a skill that is *clearly* necessary in order to have a successful and fulfilled life). Well, I had so much anxiety about the downward facing dog that after about three minutes, I got what I call the "church giggles"; you know the type: when you giggle really loud in an inappropriate place and you try to control yourself but the harder you try, the louder it gets until you squeak or snort because you have to relieve the pressure? Well they came. I was so anxious about fitting in that the laughing demons took over and I had to excuse myself.

Important **side note:** I don't know if you know this but laughing is frowned upon in yoga classes. In fact, there are three important things not to do in yoga: don't wear jeans, don't fall over on other people and don't laugh. That's it. So you can imagine how mortified I was to get the giggles. They were so bad that nobody even mentioned my Levis.

Some people say anxiety is good for you – it pushes you into flight mode and helps you accomplish things that you otherwise wouldn't. I agree with that to a certain extent. I have plenty of other stuff in my life to feel anxious about and exercise shouldn't be one of them. I submit, for your approval, a list of things that I would rather worry about than exercise:

- Driving on a freeway with teenagers texting in the cars surrounding me.
- Eating a burrito from a questionable fast food chain.
- Not being able to find a bathroom 30 minutes after said burrito has been "processed".
- Dying from a shark attack. (I don't even live near a body of water let alone one that houses sharks – but I think it illustrates my point).
- Getting shot in a dollar store parking lot. (The getting shot part doesn't give me as much anxiety as the story making the news and them using my name and everyone finding out that I frequent dollar stores. I can just hear the clerk talking to the reporter, "Yeah, she was in here just like every Tuesday. . ." oh man, I'm sweating just thinking about it.)
- Running into a teacher, professor or boss at any institution that requires bathing suits.
- Having terrible hair when I go see the stylist . . . to get my hair done. (More on this later.)
- People finding out that I jam out to 80s chick rock like 'Total Eclipse of the Heart' and 'Alone'.

I don't know that fitness will ever qualify as "fun" for me and that's just going to have to be ok. I'm not advocating sitting around on your couch (unless you are writing a book, of course) but I am questioning why exercise has to make us dread getting up in the morning. I believe in working out my body doing stuff that I love – basketball, Just Dance on the Wii and chasing small children, pretending to be some sort of animal (don't act like you haven't done it – I've found it's less scary for them when they are children that you actually know) all get my blood pumping and I think that's what matters. Long gone is the day that I feel the pressure to take up spinning. I will likely never run a marathon (can you even imagine the anxiety level if I was nervous about a 5k? I'd be puking for weeks beforehand!) or do a one-handed push-up but that's alright with me.

Here are a few other "things" about exercise or getting healthy in general that make me question all of our sanity:

1. So you can now efficiently go 30+ minutes on the elliptical trainer without feeling like you will die a certain death when you get off? Those early mornings that you've been pulling for the last eight weeks sure have paid off; the next time you are challenged to an elliptical run-off at the gym, you'll be right in it. So you can breathe better after intense cardio but here is my question: WHAT DOES THAT HAVE TO DO WITH THE SIZE OF YOUR PANTS? Nothing. So you end up not caring and eating a Twix for breakfast. Wait. You don't do that? Huh. That's awkward.

2. Diet food sucks . . . even when it's regular food. I eat chicken all the time, on or off a diet. But when I'm on a diet, it is extra dry and lacks flavor even if I cooked it the same as normal . . . simply because I've labeled it as "diet" food.   And don't even get me started on diet food that tries to taste like something else – tell me it's key lime pie yogurt, my foot. If key lime pie tasted like that in its true form, it would have to change its name to gross lime pie. Don't flavor something terrible so that it *resembles* something amazing – you just ruin both things. No matter the ratio of water to feces, once the poo is in the water, it is poo water. For me, yogurt does that to everything it tries to be like – from key lime to chocolate éclair. And don't even get me started on chocolate-flavored diet food. That's not even funny.

3. What is with the girl at the gym that wants to look like a man? It's scary and frankly, a little weird and gross. You know her. She is the one with the squirrely husband that follows her around with a towel and a water bottle, hoping that she won't decide to bench press him in front of all of his friends. She should never run in front of me at the gym because I giggle at her wide, man I have a stick up my bum, stance and I'm afraid that one day she'll hear my giggles, hit me in the face and it will all be over.

4. Exercise makes me hungry all the time. All the time. Like I can't stop being hungry whether I eat carrots or a full side of beef. Always hungry. The awkward part of that is that people probably see me always eating and then they

think "Um, she should go to the gym and not eat so much." See! How do I win? Gosh.

5. Last but certainly not least: if you ever want to hear the loudest elevator "ding" in the world, take the elevator at the gym. It probably isn't *that* loud in all reality but it sure feels like it when you are standing there. Rather than the "ding", they should just have someone come over the loudspeaker and announce that someone is about to use the elevator at the gym. "Attention all gym patrons: someone is about to engage the elevator! Please stare at them until they either cry or decide to use the stairs." It's that loud. Try it.

My advice here (if you can call it that) is to ignore the pressure to exercise like everyone else. If you like running, do it. If you like throwing heavy things in a parking lot, do it (I strictly mean this in the non-felony, empty parking lot without damaging vehicles, kind of way). Do something, anything to get you off your bum for a while and get moving – that's the point, right? If an old lady can prance her way through the park and call it a "work-out", surely you can think of something.

So says the girl who is writing a book from her couch. At least I'm swinging my legs back and forth. . .

Marriage

"Sometimes I wonder if men and women really suit each other. Perhaps they should live next door and just visit now and then." – Katharine Hepburn

So, you've landed yourself the man or woman of your dreams? Life is pretty much set. This, the only goal that seems to matter to your relatives over the age of 50, has finally been accomplished and you've proven that there actually is hope for your future. Turn in your leper card at the next family reunion and belly up to the big kids' table; you're officially in. Ah, the bliss that is sure to follow.

I had these thoughts, too. And then I realized some oddities about marriage that I feel like I need to share with you single people. Marriage is great and you should do it if you get the chance, for realzies. Just consider these little tips a little "voice of warning" so that you aren't disappointed when it isn't *all* moonlight and roses. And those of you that are already married, well, at least now you know that someone can relate.

"When you get married, I hope it's the kind of relationship where you tell each other everything!" I used to hear that advice and think what a wonderful and trust-filled environment that would be: sharing our warmest memories over cups of hot chocolate in the wee hours of the morning. Life would be just like a modern-day Dickens novel.

What they don't tell you is that when you get married, you *have* to tell each other everything. . . mostly to avoid sheer boredom; there is a lot of potential "dead air" after you get married – car travel, getting ready in the morning, Friday nights, you know, all the really mundane times when you are forced to talk to each other. You will be with this person almost as much as you were with your mom when she was still your food supply, so new material will be crucial to your success.

This is one of the main reasons that I advocate getting married later in life – you just have more stories to tell (unless you were a fantastically adventurous or rebellious child, then you should get married when you are 14. Seriously, it will turn out fine.). Even if they are boring stories, it is still fresh material and you need it as much as a stand-up comedian. That's what your single years are for, people. You need to do crazy things and make mistakes and travel so that when you get married, you have something to talk about. It's not just about squandering your money on new video games and pizza.

If you don't find ways to make your life interesting beforehand, you will quickly find yourself reaching into the far recesses of what is considered worthwhile conversation, just to avoid silence; things like "Did you see the new billboard on the freeway?" or "Our daughter pooped three times today." will become regular vernacular as you try and spark the conversational fire. As a **side note**: don't pay so much attention to billboards that you look like a drunk weaving in and out of traffic. Apparently cops hate that. Also, pay attention to the consistency of the poops – it can add a solid (or not so solid, depending on what she ate) 45 seconds to that conversational ditty.

About three years into my marriage, I realized that the "You never told me about that" statements were coming further and further apart and everything that we were reminiscing about had been discussed in substantial detail previously – same jokes, same details, same pauses for the laugh track. What was happening to us? So I had to pull out the big guns: I talked about crap I saw on YouTube. Endless supply, people. YouTube is to conversation what a spare tire is to a car: nobody wants to use it and the quality is generally crap, but it will rescue you in the unfortunate event that you need it.

The marital conversation problem compounds itself when you have an impatient spouse who, rather than letting you tell your story anyway (filling valuable dead air), interrupts you three lines in and either says "We've had this conversation" or hurriedly finishes the story for you: "…and then the teacher threw her out of class and on her way out she farted. I know." "YOU RUINED IT!"

Impatient spouses are the worst. I'm working on it, honey. I promise.

Sound effects

Speaking of good stories, one thing that I have come to enjoy about my husband telling stories is all of the sound effects that he drops into them. I never imagined that listening to a story once I was married would be so THX-ish: sound effects coming from every corner so that you feel like you are in the middle of the show. And they are good sound effects, people. Not the crappy ones like when someone drops Pez on the floor in a movie and it sounds like bullets hitting concrete.

I think that men are generally better at sound effects in stories than women but I didn't notice how terrible I was at making sound effects until my daughter hit the "What does it sound like?" stage of toddler-dom. Did you know that rockets sound the same as airplanes and fireworks? They don't? That's weird because if my daughter keeps asking me what things sound like, she won't be able to tell the difference between a slamming door and a lawnmower.

I basically have two sound effects that I make; the first sounds like something is blowing up. This is used for anything with an engine, any sort of accident, shattering glass or anything that I don't know the sound for. "What sound does a giraffe make, mommy?" Apparently it sounds like a four-car pile-up because that's all I could think of. As a **side note**: you are laughing at me right now because I don't know the sound a giraffe makes, aren't you? Well, go ahead. What sound *does* a giraffe make? Not so easy, is it? All of you future moms out there, there will come a day when you are reviewing your zoo animals and the sounds they make and the ever-debilitating giraffe will come up. You will panic and realize that you have no idea what sound a giraffe makes while your kid sits there and stares at you with disappointed eyes, like you just dropped a notch below dad on the intelligence scale. Don't panic. It's a trick question – those sneaky two-year-olds can't pull one over on us. I had to Google it and apparently adult giraffes don't make noise – you know, other than the slobbery leaf-chewing noise. Baby giraffes sometimes scream like little kids but they grow out of that. Don't worry moms; I've got your back. My work here is done.

The second sound effect that I make is for anything that shoots and it goes like this: Pew, pew, pew. Now I realize that a large shotgun does not sound like guns on a space-traveling warship AT ALL, but that's all I've got. My husband no longer lets me tell people stories after we go shooting, something about making us sound like "little girls with water guns". Go figure.

I don't own a man card

If you ask me to my face, I would still tell you that I'm the independent sort of lady that does things on her own; who needs a man to get things done while I'm around? Well apparently I do. As I look around my house while I type this, I'm realizing that I haven't hung one picture up in this entire house. Oh, I've been plenty involved in *where* to hang the pictures but physically taking the hammer and doing it, nope.

Before I got married, I owned a dilapidated house that needed a lot of fixing . . . and by "a lot" I mean it needed things done that were not "code" in the century that my house was built. You can imagine that they weren't small projects like changing a light bulb but rather tearing out walls and putting air conditioning in. It was my first house so not only did I need to make it inhabitable (and by me making it that way, I of course mean finding contractors to come and do the hard stuff – I paid them, so technically it's like me doing the work, right?). Anyway, even though I didn't install major appliances or build my deck (I don't even own a tool belt), I did a lot of work in and on that house. I tore out shrubs, I painted the kitchen, and I put together furniture, for crying out loud. I was a one-woman building machine. I felt overly-empowered, living on my own and taking care of myself at all times (with the exception of the rabies bat incident of 2006 – a story for another day). I really proved my skill in that house.

Fast-forward five years to when I got married and something strange happened; somewhere in our vows, there was a magic spell cast or something that automatically made me allergic to any work that should appear on a man card. You know, anything involving a power tool or a hammer or really anything that you would find at the Home Depot. It was like I was only doing all of that stuff before because I had to and now that I had a slave . . . er. . . . I mean a husband, my only responsibility is writing up lists of what needed to be done and criticizing crooked pictures. What happened?

I've been really feeling anxious about this lately, like maybe I need to get a hold of my independence and go do something manly like build a shelf or patch a hole in the wall. On the other hand, I don't hate that there is air conditioning in here and I can just watch our lawn get mowed once a week. What's a girl to do?

Socks everywhere

They just are. It's like while you are sleeping, the socks all get together and breed and then hide in random places like the kitchen and your car. You can't explain it – you know you never purchased that many pairs of socks for your husband but now they are there, draped over the light fixtures in the entry and you are left wondering what in the heck happened.

Another sock issue that seems to plague marriages like a bad case of chicken pox is how in the world socks end up everywhere . . . *except* the hamper. I find myself constantly asking "Hey, so when did you take your socks off by the fridge? Were you just grabbing some mayo and thought, 'Hmmm, this sandwich is probably going to taste better if I'm not wearing socks?'"

At least the fridge is far away from the hamper and finding socks near it is not nearly as mind blowing as finding socks RIGHT NEXT TO THE HAMPER. I know some of you are having sympathy and thinking, "Well, that hamper lid can be tough to open . . ." No. Open-topped hamper. There is no heavy lifting involved or struggling with hinges; it's basically the difference of six inches. "Full arm extension? Ugh. Not today. I just can't do it. I'm going to let these socks go and fall where they may." Seems logical.

Additional confusion sets in when you go to match socks up – there will *always* be a stray. Now you can't just figure out how you bought eight pair and they turned in four million socks, you now have to figure out how there are 13.5 pair coming out of the dryer. If Mensa could figure out this math problem, I'd really appreciate it.

The Relish Tray

One of the first years that we were married, we were having Thanksgiving at the in-laws and I was assigned the relish tray. I was relieved because it was a step up on the responsibility scale from "bring drinks" which meant that they didn't think I was totally incompetent so they would assign me something that couldn't totally ruin their Thanksgiving if I messed it up (sorry drink-bringers . . . it's kind of true), but it also wasn't as heavy as the mashed potatoes so there wasn't any major pressure to not mess up. It was only when the following conversation happened with a friend of mine that I realized something important:

"So, they are having me bring the relish tray so I think I'm in the clear."

"Cool. What are you going to put on it?"

Silence.

"What do you mean, 'What am I going to put on it?' The same thing my mom always. . . ."

You see it, right? Right there? MY mom. The same thing MY mom always puts on the relish tray. Cut to panicky inner monologue:

"What if their relish trays are different? What if canned-cheese-filled celery is not part of their relish tray? How ridiculous will I look showing up with cheese from a can? Let's see . . . cheese from a can. Olives from a can. Pickles from a jar. A jar! Maybe if I make them good pickles? Great, now I'm done for. Relish tray. Is this some kind of a test?"

It never even crossed my mind until that minute that my husband's family may do seemingly small things a different way and it could make a big difference. Was I living under a rock or what?

As we've been married, I've come to learn that our families do a lot of things differently, some major and others small but still noticeable. I know that "they" tell you to be on the lookout for the big things: What are their holiday traditions? Do they believe in spanking? Mayo or Miracle Whip? But it's the little things that you need to get ironed out quickly because they affect that day-to-day living. An example:

In my house growing up, everything had a proper function. You needed to kill a fly, you used a fly swatter or the occasional rolled up newspaper. You needed to pound a nail into the wall, hammer it was.

The husband's family was a little more resourceful in that they taught him to use what he had. Kill a fly? Use whatever you can find that weighs more than a fly. Need to pound a nail? Use whatever you can find that will drive the nail through sheetrock.

You see the difference? You can imagine the shock and awe on my face the first time I saw the husband use a household item for a purpose other than what it was intended. "Why? Why would you use that to kill a bug?"

"Because it was right here."

"But that's not what it's for."

"Who says?"

Silence. (Silence is my overly prideful way of admitting defeat if you haven't gathered that already.)

I'm not saying either way is the right way, they are just different. So, to help you avoid sticker shock when you find your "perfect" mate, here are a few things you are

going to want to investigate and settle before a fight –
sorry newlyweds, I mean "discussion"- ensues:

- How does their family order steak? (You say it's
  not a family thing but ask . . . see how far your
  spouse deviates from their parents. I have never
  eaten a steak on purpose cooked less than medium
  well. Why? Because that's how my parents always
  ordered it. That and because blood is gross. I
  digress.)

- Are they planners or fly-by-the-seat kind of
  people? You'll need to know whether to mail
  them invitations to things or text them 20 minutes
  beforehand.

- Do they dip Oreos in milk? If so, do they use
  their fingers or a fork? (Hygiene issues are
  HUGE.)

- What is the tidiness expectancy of the house, cars
  and yard? Follow-up: do they expect you to
  participate in achieving those goals? Second
  follow-up: how many socks do they currently own?

- Lastly, and most important, do they like peas?
  You can imagine my husband's disappointment
  when he found out that I don't and since I've
  claimed my territory in the kitchen, we will *never* be
  having them for dinner. Muwahahahaha.
  Seriously almost caused a divorce, people. Make
  sure you know.

If you can get a lock on these small but critical issues, the
rest will just fall into place. Take my word for it; these are

the only things that matter in the long run. And they say marriage is hard. Psh.

Having Kids

"Having a 2-year-old is like having a blender without a lid." –Jerry Seinfeld

I'm not even sure where to start talking about having kids; there is so much ground to cover. Do I start with the endless amounts of tissues scattered around in case their nose becomes a faucet at any second (literally any second) or how I carry around a bottle of Febreeze like I'm an old cowboy awaiting a shootout and my odor eliminator is my trusty firearm?

Maybe I'll take Julie Andrews' advice and start at the very beginning. . .

Getting chubbier by the minute.

After we got married, my husband and I decided that we wanted to have kids (that's right, I broke with my rich family tradition and decided to do things in the proper order). The idea of being a mom is something that I've thought a lot about in my life and just figured I'd be decent at. (Translation: I saw some other really crazy people having kids and not screwing them up beyond recognition, so I figured "What the heck?") So when the topic came up in my own home, I just figured it was the natural progression of things and gave the nod that I would agree to expand our family circle from two to three.

Well, like a lot of couples, it took a while for us to get pregnant. Thankfully, we didn't have the issues that some couples suffer (because I'm an anxiety-ridden nightmare on wheels) but it did take over a year to finally find out that we were going to have a baby which seems like an eternity when you are counting monthly. . . ahem.

Anyway, I had gotten on some new medication and soon thereafter, started not feeling well. Because we had tried for so long and not been successful, the last thing that I attributed my sickness to was being pregnant. Isn't it funny how your mind works? You spend your whole life hearing about morning sickness and upset stomach and being tired and all of that jazz and here I was, every pregnancy symptom in the book (my nose even grew – look it up, it's a real thing), and it didn't even cross my mind that pregnancy could be the cause. I'm smart, I swear. I just think that my pregnancy brain (it really exists – and I was a HUGE skeptic of it beforehand) kicked in early.

So here I am lying in bed feeling sick-as-a-dog while the hub is resting peacefully next to me. I have this flash of a thought that I should take a test (a pregnancy one, not the

LSAT). I tried to talk myself out of it by blaming my own terrible cooking the night before for the discomfort but I couldn't shake the thought. How bad can a person really screw up Ramen?

It's important to remind you that we had thought about having kids for over a year so I had a pretty good plan on how this would all work out: I would take a test and find out that we were pregnant. I would be overwhelmed with joy and excitement. I would then make my way to the store and develop some fantastically creative way of announcing to my amazing husband that he was going to be a dad. Maybe I'd serve him baby carrots and baby-back ribs for dinner. Aren't I so 1950's housewife-y?

So that morning, I sauntered into the bathroom to take (what I was sure was) another disappointing pee on a stick. I sat around and waited for the two minutes that the magic requires and turned it over. You can imagine my surprise and double checking when I saw two dark lines rather than one. I mean it was dark, like if the test could have just said "duh", it would have.

Two very important things happened at that moment: I did not get overwhelmed with joy and excitement. I audibly said to myself "Now what?" Luckily, and in case you were wondering, I did not have the same response as at the finish line of the 5k; the phrase "That sucks" never came into play. But I did have to sit in awe at the fact that two and half minutes could completely turn your brain around. Life's funny like that, huh? It's those two minute moments that make all the difference. I was excited (somewhere deep down in me) but I needed a minute to find it, that's all.

Secondarily, I never made it to the store. I had these grandiose visions of announcing to my husband that we were going to have a baby – I was so creative in my head. There were no baby carrots or ribs of any kind. Let's explore what actually happened:

Carlee enters stage right having just discovered that she was pregnant. Sits on the bed.

Husband: *Still half asleep.* How did it go?

Carlee: Uh, I think I'm pregnant.

What just happened?!?! You don't announce it like you are a 15-year-old telling their ex-boyfriend that his life is over! As a woman, you get one chance to get this right! It's like making sure your hair is done and you look cute when you get engaged – you've got one shot to do this so don't you blow it.

Yup, I blew it. All of those Pinterest ideas went straight out the window in the one moment in my life when I had no idea what to say. There would be no handmade t-shirt, no fancy dinner. My daughter's history started with the most eloquent thing I could think of at that moment: "Uh, I think I'm pregnant." (In my head, my voice when I said this sounded really lazy and manly and I feel like it adds a touch of class to the whole thing so if you could read that again in the manliest voice you can muster, I'd appreciate it. It's worth the laugh, I promise.)

So . . . we are having a baby. Things won't change that much, right? I mean, we will make our kid fit into our lives – they will go where we go and do what we do, just like a stuffed animal. That reality lasted, well, until the next time I threw up. Things would never be (or taste) the same.

I made my way to my doctor's office to confirm that I was growing a human, which they did. Bring on the doctor's appointments. (And seriously – could there be any more appointments? If I could have earned rewards points or something for each visit, I would have either scored a free week at a plush hotel or round-trip tickets to some exotic locale. Frequent customer does not even begin to describe it).

All of my life, I was excited to interact with my OB when I was pregnant – it sounds weird but I always dreamed that she would come skating in on her roller shoes and clapping and smiling because she was so excited that I was preggers. Picture Martin Short in "Father of the Bride". I thought we'd smile and talk about how cute my kid was, even when it looked like a lizard. Yes, this is how it was going to be – just like on TV.

This was not what went down. My doc came in and basically laid down the law – "be healthy, eat better, exercise, rest. Be better. You can't mess up your kid at this stage so live your life like normal. Oh and here are some pills to hopefully help with the sickness. See you in a few weeks."

"Um, you didn't clap. And your scrubs don't have little crayons on them. You are clearly not my doctor." Or so I initially thought. Just like the rest of my life, I thought I knew what I wanted but in reality, it was not what was best for me. Life = 10. Carlee = 0.

I'm what some might call, um, a ball of nervous energy. EVERYTHING makes me nervous. Everything. So, you can imagine that on a nervous scale of one to ten, growing a human is like a 46. I was sure that every time I sat up quickly, I had given my baby some sort of developmental defect. Nervous wreck did not even begin to describe me during this time. Nervous wreck was me on a really good day . . . with puppies.

If it weren't for my amazingly to-the-point doc (who probably wasn't as blunt as I remember now – I was nervous, give me a break), I never would have survived pregnancy. If I had gotten what I wanted (you know, Dr. Fun on the skates) I would have spent the entire time wondering if there were actually issues with my baby but Positive Polly just didn't want to deliver the bad news. Instead, my doc always delivered the news whether I wanted to hear it or not. For example, I did NOT want to hear that I shouldn't be eating breakfast burritos three times a week when I woke up and was starving (just as a **side note**, this *could* have happened like five times a week so I like to think that I was practicing SOME restraint). But she told me to stop it anyway because there were better things to eat.

The next nine months or so (I say "or so" because "9 months" and "40 weeks" don't match up. Do the math. There are four extra weeks tagged on there somewhere which wouldn't seem like a big deal except that they feel like they are tagged onto the end when you feel like a beached whale – they are a HUGE deal) were just the best time of my life. (Re-introduce the sarcasm font). I just had the best time throwing up and not sleeping.

Someone made the horrific mistake of telling me that once I hit 12 weeks, I'd feel tons better. So on the morning of my twelfth week, I woke up ready for my amazing transformation. In my mind, the whole pregnancy process was so weird anyway that I did not discount the possibility that a barf switch would be flipped somewhere and I'd be healed like a parishioner at one of those backwoods revivals.

I sat up, stretched a bit, smiled and threw up. LIARS! Clearly, the devil had taken over my body and I was destined to throw up every day until I died. So much for the twelfth-week relief period.

So, I threw up and grew a human for 40 weeks and did what thousands of women do every day – I had a baby. Talk about shaking you right to your core. I knew I was in trouble when on my first night as a mom, I hastily made my way to the hospital nursery (I think my gown was closed?) at four o-clock in the morning and cried to the nurse that I needed to see my mini-me. My independence, as I knew it, was over.

When you find out that you are pregnant, and I suppose even beforehand for some people, you start imagining the kind of parent that you are going to be – smart and funny, kind and caring, loving and patient. In my case, I started thinking about the kind of parent I wouldn't be – like all those "idiots" I would see in stores and restaurants and driving that were just so unprepared and couldn't seem to control their kids. "Get a grip, people! You are the parent! You are in charge! Be prepared and don't let that kid control you!"

Then I had a kid and every parenting pre-judgment that I had went straight out the window, leading me to this very important, 12-step-sponsored moment:

I'd like to formally apologize to all of those parents that I called 'idiots'. And, to make amends, I would like to publicly highlight all of those things that I swore I would never do along with a timeline of when reality set in and I became "one of you".

Pre-kid: "You look ridiculous riding in back of the car and being chauffeured by your spouse just so that your kid remains calm. Seriously, if you are prepared, you should never have to ride in the back. And if my kid was crying, I'd just let them cry it out."

Reality: There is nothing more nerve damaging than knowing you are still 30 minutes away from your destination and your child is screaming so loud that you are pretty sure the windshield is going to crack. Not only can you not handle the screaming because you are likely going someplace that you had to give yourself a pre-departure pep-talk to attend in the first place, but the prospect of doing it for another 30 minutes makes you want to pull your eyebrows out one by one for a sense of relief. At that point, a car becomes a self-contained torture device equal to Chinese water torture.

Reality happened for me in a major way when my daughter was about 3 months old: "Pull over!"

"Where?"

"I don't care! At this point, stop in the middle of the road! Just stop! I need to change seats. I'm pretty sure her head just rotated all the way around."

So what did I do? I became a one-man puppet show/feeding machine/peek-a-boo playing back seat companion.

And that was the end of that.

Pre-kid: "You look ridiculous – there is a mustard handprint on your shirt. Can't you tell when your kids have sticky fingers and keep them from touching your clean clothes? Let's look presentable, people. Why do moms always look disheveled when they have little kids?"

Reality: I should have slapped myself when I had this thought. Seriously – what was I thinking? No! You can't tell when your kids have sticky fingers because .07 seconds ago, they were completely clean and ready to head out the door! There wasn't even *time* for them to get sticky . . . but they did. And just like sometimes you don't immediately notice cilantro in your own teeth after a big meal, you also don't notice that when your kid is crying on your shoulder, clear snot is being propelled into your hair.

I'm going to be honest that I've looked like a disheveled mess since the day I had my first daughter. But the reality of just how naïve I was about it hit me when my daughter was roughly a year old. I put on a nice sweater (that I rarely wore – remember, I've looked like a mess for a year) to head to a client meeting. I did a quick glance in the mirror, excited to see some semblance of the business professional I once was, and headed to my meeting. As I was chatting with the client, I casually crossed my arms and put my hand on my opposite arm. I felt an embarrassingly cold sweat start as I thought "Um, why does my sweater feel crunchy?" I lost whatever was discussed for the next minute or so as I casually examined the back of my arm only to discover, to my horror, that my sweater was covered in crushed up (what I think was) cookie. "Hi, I'm here in dirty clothes for our meeting." Oh. My. Gosh.

How did this happen? Didn't I look in the mirror? Have I even worn this sweater since I had my daughter? (You'll be glad to know I had.) When did we have cookies? All of these questions circulated through my head until I finally realized that "nice clothes" were about to take on a whole new meaning. Nice clothes = clothes that the stains don't really show up on. Multi-colored fabrics were my new bff.

Pre-kid: "Seriously . . . is it that hard to be prepared? Why would you ever leave the house without food, diapers, wipes and a change of clothes? That's what the diaper bag is for. Your kid should never look homeless, smell terrible or be bored or hungry as long as you are an organized, prepared parent."

Reality: I couldn't even type this section without apologizing out-loud to the Greek Goddess of Motherhood. All I have to say about this is YOU JUST DON'T KNOW! Oh, you can be prepared with crackers but what happens when one day, your kid just spits them at you like you've fed them dog feces? They liked the crackers every day until today – why would today be any different? Oh, it is. Today they think the crackers taste like poop in a bag. They will like them again, eventually. But until then, don't you plan on just crackers to hold off starvation. Crying ensues. Bad mom.

Diapers? I was sure I just re-loaded the bag with like thirty. But two of them ripped mid-change yesterday and the babysitter forgot to tell you that there were (apparently) 27 severe blow-outs. So now, we sit, smelly and alone and 20 miles or a million dollars away from a new pack (That's how much they are at the grocery store, kids. A MILLION dollars. Talk about birth control – nobody tells you that business in high school). What happened?

Reality really set in one Sunday at church when our daughter was about 10 months old. She had what could only qualify as a rotting carcass in her diaper and her sweet father took her to the bathroom to change her. After about ten minutes, he brought her back in where I was sitting, all wrapped up nice and cozy in her blanket. As I went to grab her, he quickly informed me that the blanket was no longer serving its dictionary-assigned purpose; the blanket had officially become our baby's new dress/skirt/pants/whatever attire you deem as appropriate for church - you can use your imagination. Apparently the carcass had crawled its way out of the diaper and through three layers of clothing. My daughter looked either completely ridiculous or could have been the poster child for a baby sorority toga party. Why didn't I bring an extra set of clothes? Because YOU DON'T KNOW!

Pre-kid: "I hate when parents use their kid as an excuse to not be social anymore. Just bring them with you. Bedtimes aren't that big of a deal – you should raise your kids to be flexible with sleep and behave in public. And if not, you just pull them aside and tell them to behave. I'll never leave a dinner/party/social event early because of some crazy kid melt-down."

Reality: I can't even remember the last time that I agreed to attend an event that started after 7:00. I don't even know what that looks like anymore. I'm like Cinderella . . . before her curfew got extended. At promptly 7:00, my ball gown turns into pajama pants and my car no longer starts. The sun even sets later than that but I don't care – if it can't be mistaken for afternoon, it doesn't exist.

To this point, I've left all kinds of events early, either because of some sort of sleep schedule or because of a satanic meltdown. What pre-parents don't understand is that there is an approximate 4 minute timeframe between your child being 'ok' and their head detaching and turning a full circle in some sort of demonic outrage. I'm serious – 4 minutes. Moms can just look at their baby and know when the clock has started – like some sort of fatal Olympic race except if you don't get moving, you don't just lose, they set the track on fire.

When it's close to bed time and a mom says "We better get going," or, in the more urgent, the-countdown-has-begun tone, "We have to go," you just can't take offense. In fact, I would tell you that your smartest move is to help pack up the diaper bag and get her in the car just as fast as possible – that is unless you want to perform some sort of cleansing ritual on your house to get the bad spirits out because Crazy Baby is about to make an appearance.

I complain about how difficult it is but being a mom is easily the best thing I've ever done – it's the second time I've been able to boss someone around and really feel justified (that's also why I got married. Jokes, jokes). It's completely fulfilling and terrifying to see a little person with your mannerisms and attitude traipsing around like a three-foot sponge and soaking up all that you have to offer; that's when you really start questioning your daily choices. Life (as you can see) will never be the same . . . and it's fantastic.

The Clothes Make the Man

"If you have to ask if clothing item is a dress or a top, it is always a top." –Tim Gunn

Ever notice that you can look put together 80% of the time and never see anyone that you know, but the second you are working from home and have to run to the store really quick so you slip on some gym shorts and a grungy 'Spartan Spirit' t-shirt and don't comb your hair, you see everyone that you haven't seen in over a year and make a killer, mildly musty impression on them? "Why are you here?!?" They now think you are jobless and homeless, not just because you smell funky but because you are buying a half gallon of one percent and a box of donut holes. "Yes, this is my meal this week." Funny, life. Funny.

I hate getting dressed. Don't take this the wrong way – I'm not saying this in the creepy, "we walk around naked when we can" kind of way. I mean in real clothes – ones with buttons and zippers and ruffles and stuff. Nothing says comfort to me like this one word: drawstring. Am I right? If it were socially acceptable, I'd wear comfy pants and a hoodie everywhere I went; church, job interviews, the Met - they'd all be more enjoyable in the touch, the feel of oversized cotton. There is a freeing feeling in knowing that if your clothes somehow caught on fire, you wouldn't need to fight a potentially jammed zipper in order to free yourself from the inferno. (Have I mentioned that I worry a lot about unnecessary things? Add this to the list right under shark attacks on dry land.).

I know that you are thinking that comfy pants and a hoodie are just irrational – what happens when it's hot? I'm not completely unreasonable. Basketball shorts and a t-shirt can serve as an appropriate substitute where necessary.

Based on this, you can imagine that I have incredible fashion sense. After all, I basically just admitted that zippers are hard. I'm a self-admitted slacker when it comes to dressing to the nines so you'd have to imagine that something is really, really wrong when even I, the frump-girl of Clothing Lane, can notice some impropriety in other people's clothing selections.

Let's start with the obvious, shall we:

Fit

Even though they make that piece of clothing in your size, you should always ask yourself, "Should they?" I can emphatically tell you that the answer in most cases is "no"

– particularly if the words "Lycra" or "Spandex" or "Polyester" are written on the label with a number larger than 10% next to them. If the material you are about to buy could double as a parachute or other life-saving device, make sure that it's not about to resemble one when you wear it to dinner; Which leads me to my second, more general rule of thumb:

Be wary of the word "stretchy" as it pertains to your clothing. Generally, these fabrics carry no warranty that they will actually "stretch" the body part they are covering; they simply imply that they will stretch AROUND said body part and, in most cases, pull it to a place that it shouldn't be. "Stretchy" is a warning label for us chubby kids – the direct translation is "Not a good idea. Please move on to a more structured fabric."

Failure to comply with these easy, yet critical, fit rules can often lead to a tragedy that I like to call the Sausage Casing Syndrome. You've seen it and winced at it before, I'm sure. Time and time again someone walks into the room and their clothes immediately make you think of deli meat – like some butcher magician just packed 18 ounces of whatever kind of meaty filler into an eight ounce rubberized casing. You know that all the meat is there but it's a mystery how it all fit.

The problem with this syndrome is that it isn't always apparent before you leave the house so it is important to do some testing before you leave the privacy of your closet. A couple of weeks ago, I pulled out this blue shirt that I used to love and slipped (OK, pulled) it down over me. I stood in front of the mirror and actually felt pretty good that it "fit" again. All of the signs were there: it covered everything that it needed to and I could breathe. (Pretty weak costuming approval criteria, huh? Remember, my nickname is "drawstring".) Anyway, I brushed my teeth and finished doing all of my other standing-up morning routine duties as assigned. (As you might be expecting, that "standing-up" notation is going to become important in three, two, one. . .)

As I got in my car to leave for work, the shirt started to feel just a smidge tighter than it had all morning. "I didn't eat a big breakfast," I thought to myself, "It must just be in my head." And I headed off to work.

Well, two hours into the day, I was just this side of a panic attack, feeling like my blue shirt was sucking the life right out of me like some bad 80s sci-fi alien. Operating under my delusional excitement that morning that the shirt fit again, I failed to realize that if anyone wanted me to reach anything over my head or sit for an extended period of time (did I mention I work at a desk?), I was hosed. "I can't move my arms! I can't breathe. And suddenly I feel a craving for a hot dog."

Reality sunk in quickly and I realized that the last time I had worn this shirt, I was apparently twelve years old and had less of a hunkering for chocolate. Sausage. Casing.

I realize now that I failed to go through an important clothing rite of passage that morning, leaving me in a lurch for the remainder of my work day: the sit test.

Have you ever noticed that when you sit down, things push up and out and in all sorts of directions that they don't when you are standing? (Anyone with less than 10% body fat can skip this part – I can't relate to you anyway). This realization is my justification for the sit test.

If you are about to walk out of your house with an article of clothing that feels "comfortable-ish", I implore you to sit down in it for five minutes before you commit to a day-long endeavor. If, in that five minutes you can't breathe regularly, hear some sort of tearing fabric, feel the pain of crushed ovaries or loose feeling in your legs or arms, it's probably best that you head back to the dressing room and re-think today's costume. I promise that if you are feeling it, other people are seeing it.

Now these rules don't just apply to your everyday clothing – accessories are not exempt from standardized testing, folks. I once wore this lovely (albeit slightly painful) accessory that I now refer to as my Chinese bracelet of death; wearing it for a few minutes was no skin off my back (or my arm, as the case may be) but every few minutes for the next couple of hours, I'd feel this sharp pain in my wrist, like my new bracelet had also come with a complementary session of acupuncture (how many racial stereotypes can I make in one paragraph, I ask you? But seriously, I don't think it was a coincidence). As I *finally* took the bracelet off, I noticed that the spectacular chainmail that made up my shiny new pet was not closed properly – it, in fact, was like little needles stabbing my arm! So, feeling relieved that I had found the source of my pain, I did what any girl would do and put the bracelet back on until I got home. . . it matched my outfit.

Why do we do this to ourselves!?

Can we all just agree that no matter how cute, if you cannot leave your house without already having multiple fights with your clothing, you need to surrender immediately? Discard the clothing that is bothering you because I can promise you this with 100% certainty:

IT WILL BOTHER YOU ALL DAY.

That is all.

Some call it "original"

When costuming, ask yourself: Have I seen anyone else in anything similar to this clothing item? No? Put it back and walk away. I know that you were thinking that I was going to give you some rant about originality and being yourself but I'm not. Why be the Guinea Pig? If you see it in mass production it means someone else already ran the risk and passed the test. There is a reason why white shirts and the little black dresses are called "classic".

Have you ever noticed that it's all of the fruit balls that wear some one-of-a-kind designer dress to the Oscars that get pinned to the "Worst Dressed" list? It's never the girls that wear the black dress or a subtle navy blue strapless number; it's always the girl who thinks it would be fantastic to wear a swan draped around her neck or a dress made entirely out of cold cuts that get the wrath of those lists. Very rarely does it ever turn out well – as soon as the red carpet starts on television, you can almost audibly hear stylists around all of Hollywood packing their bags. Guinea Pigs, I tell you. It's a scary place to live. Speaking of animals:

Raaaarrrrr (if you are picturing a tiger, my subtitle worked. If you are confused, I blame the editor.)

When buying animal prints, ask the following question: When wearing this, will I at ALL resemble the animal whose skin this is supposed to represent? If the answer is a resounding "Heck yes!" and you feel the need to purr at yourself or make a sassy air-scratching motion, immediately discard your outfit and promise that you'll start over, from scratch. . . maybe you should even shower again.

Animal prints are meant to barely remind on-lookers of animals, not have them cower in fright that one is actually charging toward them. This is a good rule of thumb not just when trying to decide what animal prints to wear but exactly how much of said print to wear. Leopard-print shoes, ok. Leopard-print shirt, pants, shoes and bag: not ok. Oh and lastly, please don't mix animal species when dressing. Have you ever seen a cheetah breed with a snake anywhere outside of the state fair? Me neither. Let's keep it that way.

I'm going to polish off this turd with exemplary style; I can handle a lot of fashion faux pas in my day-to-day living but one thing that drives me bananas is going to professional conferences, conducting job interviews or just everyday work interactions and seeing what people deem as appropriate job attire. So, let's start hashing through how to be less dumb in our professional dress, shall we? I'll make this brief:

- Regardless of how "hip" you are trying to be, your tennis shoes don't go with your suit. Ever. You automatically lose ten credibility points the second someone sees this infraction. They think to themselves, "He could be cool to go bowling with." Good statement to have running through someone's head when you want to be hired as their accountant, eh? You aren't five – there is no excuse for it. Even cheap stores have dress shoes. Invest in a pair.

- When purchasing a dress to wear to a business dinner, the front should have no slippery access points; nothing should ever "accidentally" fall out or peek out or poke out while you are at dinner. There should be no visible zippers and especially not two zippers that run in opposite directions. Your dress should not have awkward cutouts or anything that would make your dinner companions think about having you for an entrée. I'm not saying you should dress like you are delivering a message from an ultra-conservative religious group – that is equally as creepy; but there is a broad spectrum between sister wife and street walker that would be considered appropriate business attire. Choose wisely.

- Speaking of dresses and skirts – they can, in fact, be too short, no matter how great your legs are. Rule of thumb: more thigh should be covered than showing. Long gone is the excuse that you just have long legs – we all know what you are trying to accomplish. Get in line, we all need a raise.

- Casual Friday does not give you free-reign to wear clothes that would frighten young children. If your "normal" dress tends to err on the side of death, it is best keep your white makeup in the car regardless of what the company-wide memo says. Don't bring it into work. If you want to express yourself to your coworkers, do it on Facebook – we all know that's a safe-haven? #thisistherealme

- With the exception of a minor few that have an acute shoulder deformity, what purpose to shoulder pads really serve? What kind of illusion are you trying to pull off? Are you planning to take a nap at your desk and you need something cushy to rest your head on? I must have missed that passage in business school that said "In order to look like a tougher boss, heighten and sharpen your shoulders; people will now respect you." I know that natural shoulders don't come in that shape unless you play in the NHL so we know you bought your pant suit in 1984. We aren't intimidated.

- Lastly - even if your cruise does leave to the Bahamas in 48 hours and even if you could get a screaming deal on corn rows *before* you leave, don't do it and certainly don't come to work like that. There is nothing offensive or inappropriate about this – I just think it's so funny and you'll likely be made fun of for at least six months by your co-workers. (I'd like to take this moment to issue a challenge to be on the lookout for the early vacation starters at your work – if you see them, send me a picture. I'll blog about it. So funny.)

And finally:

When Tucking. . .

When tucking a shirt in, do you tuck into the pants or all the way down into the underwear? Now I'm pretty sure I know the socially correct answer to this (nobody is going to **admit** to the underwear), but I want to you to look into the real, honest truth because I continually see evidence that would lead me to believe that this underwear tucking may happen on a regular basis for a lot of people. And if you DO admit to the underwear tucking, is it the added security of the elastic band that entices you so? Does it stay tucked better that way or something because I can't get over the 'sick' factor.

It's a sad day for fashion.

Work

*"Work is hard. That's why it's called 'work'.
Otherwise it would be called 'Toys and Candy'".*

-Carlee

So, I've had a big-kid job for about ten years now. I hate when people refer to these jobs as 'professional' jobs – like you have to have a degree in order to be a professional at anything. I was a professional at a lot of things, long before I got a degree. In fact, I think I was seven or so the first time I was told I was a professional smart mouth and I wasn't even in advanced placement classes or anything. Psh, who needs a degree?

In addition, I know a whole slew of people who got their degree and I would, in no way, qualify them as a 'professional'. These are the people that I ignore and pretend that I never saw their invitation on LinkedIn.

As I've continued to watch youngsters (I can call you that now because I've crossed another decade marker) come into the workforce, I'm realizing that their expectations about what work is are very different than mine were (And continue to be). My pre-game pep talk went something like this:

"Well, you get up early and sit in traffic in the car you bought in high school because you can't afford anything else yet. Then you get to work, sit at your desk, do some stuff and then take a lunch. Or sometimes you don't because you are busy. And then you work more and then you go home. You do that every day for thirty years. It sucks for everyone but be glad that you have a job. You are lucky to be working."

Good times – glad I got my degree for this merry-go-round!

On the contrary, I feel like kids are getting a slightly different version of this pep talk these days, one that is making it very hard to like them at work. Their's (I believe) goes something like this:

"Well, just take the train to the office. That way you can sleep and listen to your music on the way in. When you get there, just act smarter than everyone and they will respect you. You'll be getting your work done fast enough to check social media several times in the morning – be sure to post about how lame work is and how dumb your boss is. They don't check social media because they are old – you'll be fine. Take a long lunch but be sure to tell everyone that you won the ping pong tournament in the break room and that's why you are late getting back. Mid-afternoon, go ask your boss for a raise. When he asks why, just tell him that you've been there for six months – they basically *have* to give you one when you've been there that long. After that, leave a little early so that you can play on the company softball team – they love it when you are involved outside of the office. If you hate it, you can just quit. I'd be looking for another job anyway, just in case it's not what you expect."

You'll recognize these kiddos when they walk into the office on their first day wearing socks that cost more than your entire outfit and immediately complain that there are no sushi places within walking distance. (Apparently the sushi from the gas station doesn't count? Some people are such snobs.)

You aren't above this job . . . or below this job . . . you just are this job.

I have real issues with entitlement when it comes to work, mostly from those expensive-sock-wearing kids that I referenced above; well them and a good portion of my extended family.

I particularly hate it when the "I'm too good for this" attitude shows up on a job that you applied for *and* took. On occasion, I'll run into someone who must vehemently hate their job based on the way they are throwing chicken nuggets in my daughter's kid's meal. I wonder "Did someone force you into this? What dictator forced you to make said chicken nuggets? You should have slapped whoever filled out the application for this job for you and *made* you work here."

I'm not saying that serving chicken nuggets to a bunch of hungry kids is the most glamorous job (wait until you do the same thing and don't get paid – what's up, moms!) but didn't you sign up for this? I mean I know it was a tough decision between taking this job and being Miss America but . . . seriously. You took this job. Be glad you have one. Stop acting like you are too good for it and appreciate being at work. (And if you could stop missing my bun entirely with my hamburger, I'd appreciate it).

The same thing applies in the corporate world as it does when "large size it" is a part of your daily routine. Work can be equally frustrating for ivy-league 22 year-olds that "have to start somewhere" (I'm not one of those – I was a local-college-er that was "thankful to not be cleaning toilets" after college). The problem is that you start your job, having just spent four million dollars on your upper-division text books that clearly tell you how it's going to be in the workplace; those end-of-chapter case studies are real life and set you up to hit the ground running. What they don't tell you is that they are someone else's real life and you aren't likely to experience an industry-changing scenario like that until you are 40. Your reality is that you will actually be doing mindless spreadsheets and extreme sessions of note taking for the next eight months. If you're lucky, someone will ask for your opinion around month one or two . . . and then laugh because you thought they were serious. I'm not a buzzkill, just a realist.

My point is this: Nobody is too good for any job. Period. The most respectable thing that you can do for yourself is to *have* a job, whatever it is. If you think it is more respectable to "hold out for the management position that you deserve" and collect no paycheck than to take a job making sandwiches, you are nutty. Particularly if that "hold out" lasts for 12 years.

Who's the boss?

Bosses are a tricky work subject because in many instances, they are terrible. I've been lucky enough in my career to work for some pretty awesome bosses . . . and some pretty terrible ones . . . so I feel qualified to give some insight here.

Everyone takes a job (at least in part) because the person that interviewed them is "amazing" and will be "so great to work for". Of course they are! You went in there NEEDING A JOB so I'm pretty sure you slapped on those rose-colored glasses and saw what you wanted to see in your potential paycheck signer. They were "so funny" and "really knowledgeable" and "really appreciated my resume and eight years of transcripts." Working for said interviewer just "feels right". Sound familiar?

So when your new boss fails to meet your expectations on the third day that you are employed, is it really their fault? Not if your expectation was that you'd have a raise by then and a donut on your desk every morning because you are doing so well. Oh, does nobody else expect that? Weird. Because I've been thoroughly disappointed several times (mostly about the donut).

You see, you can't put unfair expectations on your boss and then complain when they don't meet them – it's that same speech you gave to your parents in high school but now you need to be the one hearing it. Bosses are regular people who have worked for a long time (or are extraordinarily smart and still 12 years old) and are trying to keep their jobs, too. How do they do that? By hiring smart people to make them look good. (If it ever crossed your mind that you were hired to be groomed to eventually be in your boss' office, smack yourself. That's not how the circle of life works.) Once you can see that's what they are doing, your patience should increase.

On the other hand, some bosses are *only* bosses because they have worked at a place of business since Moses was a boy. These kinds of bosses are the worst – they are entitled and mean and generally not very smart. They are only your boss because they know the entire history of the company and they keep the turnover rate at a reasonable level.

I have a strict rule in my life that everyone should follow so bosses, listen up: you can be mean and smart or you can be nice and dumb. Those are the options. If you are mean and smart, at least your employees will respect your brain and fear you for it. They may not like you personally (bowling is definitely out) but they will fear you and that's important. If you are nice and dumb, nobody will want to point out your stupidity because you are so nice to them and it will make happy hour really awkward because they are worried you won't buy everyone drinks. People don't fear your mind but they want to eat lunch at your table. You're okay too.

The bosses that choose to be jerks and have no backing for said tyranny (the ones that violate my rule and choose to be mean and dumb at the same time) deserve to be taken down. I encourage you to do whatever you need to do to "out" them for the idiots that they are and take them out. I submit, for your reading pleasure, a list of all of the bosses that I've run into that fit this category:

Just kidding. I wouldn't actually list them here. Not because I want to save them even a shred of embarrassment but because I'm still working on plans to humiliate them one day and I don't want to spoil the surprise.

When traveling. . .

"I have found out that there ain't no surer way to find out whether you like people or hate them than to travel with them." –Mark Twain

Remember that exciting world when you were younger? When your parents told you that the family was going on a trip? It didn't really matter where – my mom could have classified a visit to the grocery store as a 'trip' and it would have taken on the majesty of a princess castle. I didn't care – a trip meant freedom, a trip meant exploration, a trip meant no chores.

Will work for adventure

As I've gotten older, traveling has lost a bit of its luster. I mainly attribute it to the fact that no matter how long the flight, the pretzels are always the same. I remember being little and flying across the country for the first time – after sleeping for a couple of hours on the empty row of three chairs, I was awakened by a smiling steward with a bowl of

101

cold cereal and a banana for my morning consumption. These days, the only cold cereal that I can get on a flight is in a hermetically sealed box with a notarized note from the manufacturer that it has not, in fact, been tampered with. In addition, the only smiles that I seem to get from any of the flight attendants is a sarcastic one right before they tell me "no".

I think I've only become a jaded traveler since I started traveling for work. The first time I went on a business trip, we were going over a few days for a conference. I, in all of my naiveté, arrived at the airport and checked my bag. ABORT! ABORT! First rule of business travel – you don't check a bag. Unless you are being sent to Dubai for a two week meeting/camel riding adventure where packing poses an issue, you make it fit in a carry-on. Always. It doesn't matter if you are going for 3 days or three minutes, you make it fit. Add that to your book Harvard Business School. That is the real meat and potatoes of an MBA.

I learned this lesson quickly as my bosses and I exited the plane and they headed straight for the car rental bus . . . without me. My inner monolog: "Um, uh, bag, clothes, not important, homeless at meeting, need, wait!" I scampered like the puppy I was and let my boss know that I had to get my bag. If eye rolls could kill a person, that one would have done me in like a bad case of the plague. It was awful. I was mortified to stand there for what seemed like an eternity, flanked by two executives, waiting for my properly-packed bag to make its way down that dumb ramp. How big was this airport? Was my bag going through reverse security? Did the drug dogs respond poorly to my Aqua Net? I honestly think that there had to be some discussion about just leaving me and making me take a cab; I was lucky it was the recession and we were there trying to make a buck, not lose 100, so they had to wait. Needless to say, I was berated for the rest of the trip, by me.

In my mind I quickly became a business-travel veteran: purchasing the right luggage, printing my boarding pass before getting to the airport, ignoring the people that I worked with at the airport until I absolutely had to discuss something work-related. (I don't do this but if this has happened to you and you cried all the way to your meeting because you were sure your bosses hated you, don't fret. Apparently it's normal for them to turn their heads away from you when you pass by them in first class and mutter 'lowlife' under their breath. It's cool. Get comfy in coach and know that your job is no more in jeopardy than it was prior to this little excursion.) All of these seemingly insignificant moves are critical to corporate travel survival, so take note.

Aren't you glad you are reading all of these 'how to survive work travel' gems? So the next time a rookie makes his way onto the scene and asks if you (his travel companions) brought your swimming suites because the hotel looks like it has a pretty sweet pool, you can just shake your head and smile. You're welcome.

That's an upgrade?

One thing that has always driven me crazy when I travel is the word "upgrade"; apparently my long-standing relationship with this word is built on a lie. You see, I've always thought that upgrade meant some sort of change, resulting in a *better* situation than was originally intended. In the hospitality industry, however, it simply means a change . . . period. Let's take a look at a couple of examples, shall we?

You are boarding a flight and the stewardess sees that you are a million months pregnant and moves you to a first-class seat. This, in my book, is an upgrade. (And it's an upgrade of the best kind – a free one).

On the contrary, you are getting your seat assignment from the counter even though you are sure you selected an aisle seat in the exit row when you originally purchased your ticket. Now, magically, your boarding pass says "See counter" instead of "12C" like it should. After you go to said counter, the airline employee says to you "Well, it's a good thing you got here early. You're lucky; we're able to get you on the flight."

"Wait, what?"

"Yeah, this flight is oversold by 100 seats and *luckily* you got here in time to get a seat. Here is your assignment – 38B."

Because you've flown before, you quickly recognize the letter "B" as the airline translation of "uncomfortable" and have visions of a phlegmy old man on your left and a body-builder on your right, dancing in your head. You also notice that row 38 doesn't normally exist on these planes so they might as well have listed "toilet jump seat" as your new seat assignment.

The new assignment isn't what gets you though – it's that word the airline employee used, that word "lucky". What is that? Don't look at me like I've clearly never flown before and you are doing me a favor (aka giving me an upgrade) and I should be praising you for getting me on this plane! No! I chose 12C, lady. I did. I did! "Lucky". No.

Another example:

You are traveling with your coworkers and have each booked a room at a hotel. Clearly, you pick the standard room with the king size bed. You might as well sprawl for one night, right?

As you go to check in, the hotel desk clerk hands you your keys and says "Good news, we were able to upgrade you to a room with a view and a Jacuzzi tub." That is an upgrade! On the contrary. . .

As you go to check in, the hotel desk clerk hands you your keys and says "Good news, we were able to upgrade you to a room with two queen beds."

"Um, I actually just want what I booked – one bed, a big bed. No "upgrade" necessary."

"Well, unfortunately all of those rooms are taken so we are happy to offer you the upgrade to two beds without any extra charge."

"Well fantastic. I was hoping I could have one bed for me and one for my laptop. Who wants a big bed when you can sleep on a smaller one, as long as there is another bed in the room, three feet away that you can stare at? So, it's this or the lobby couches? Cool. Thanks for the upgrade."

This is the part where a normal person would go to their room and sleep in one bed and move on. Not me. If I get an upgrade, I take advantage. I upgrade myself all over that extra bed – pulling the blanket off, adding pillows. . . I think of all of the things I can use my upgrade to do while I'm in there all by my upgraded self; that extra bed becomes the TV-watching bed, the suitcase holder bed, the accidentally spill my drink bed (you know, if it randomly happens). Man, they are right. This IS an upgrade.

Just because I love making lists, let me tell you a few other things that are also not upgrades when you travel (you know, for clarity sake):

Shared bathrooms at a hotel

Pretzels instead of peanuts (everyone knows that peanuts are the superior snack food on a plane)

Weekly sheet washings (the hotel isn't the only thing "going green")

No windows in your room (they may sell this to you as a 'natural retreat where you can get in-touch with your surroundings'. Don't fall for it.)

A leaking shower ceiling. "Actually, it doesn't really feel like a waterfall at all – it just feels like a leaky ceiling."

Coming Home

Easily the worst part about traveling anywhere is the trip home. Even when you take a short work trip, that last leg home can feel like an eternity. Who knew it actually took 47 hours to fly across the country? And why is it on the way home that they give you a layover in the opposite direction of your actual destination? Like it makes perfect sense to put me down in Virginia when I'm flying from Kentucky to California? I didn't exactly *excel* at the Geography Olympiad but based on my elementary knowledge, something here is amiss.

Coming home is particularly difficult when you've been on an actual vacation and not just a work trip – you know the kind where you are in a warm climate and sleep into the double digits of late morning? When I come home from these trips, I have all sorts of messed up notions that the service and relaxation that I experienced at a resort should continue after I return. Some things I've noticed:

- Work is still there and your boss expects you to do it. Work on vacation usually consists of walking up two flights of stairs on your way back from the pool or figuring out that daunting Sudoku puzzle that just didn't seem to come out right. Now, there is typing and emails and spreadsheets and

107

ugh, I'm exhausted even talking about it. I think I need to lie down.

- Speaking of . . . naps. I can basically sleep everywhere on vacation: in the chair by the pool, on a boat, on the couch in the lobby, at the dinner table . . . really, wherever. When I get home, I can't seem to fall asleep anywhere – particularly at work. No matter how tired I *clearly* am or how many post-it notes I leave around stating how tired I am, there is always something or someone bugging me. I tried sneaking into the mother's lounge to nap for a minute during lunch one time when I returned from vacation – did you know that you need a key? What goes on in there that would require a key? I wanted to nap bad enough that I actually thought about a minor criminal offense (stealing said key) just to sleep. That and to figure out what is going on in there that would warrant a key.

- When you come back from vacation, do you find yourself waiting for a bar maid to pass your cubicle and ask you what you'll have to drink? I do. And when I finally asked the secretary to get me a Pina colada, she said some things that were NOT very nice. It probably didn't help that I was out of tip money.

- Besides my drinks on demand (which I still don't see as unreasonable), I'm still waiting to open my linen closet and see my bath towel folded like a swan. I've been informed by my family that this is a "ridiculous expectation" and "requires training" and a bunch of other lame excuses; apparently "Google it" doesn't resolve their hesitation to go down this road.

- Every day on vacation, I eat way better than I do at home, particularly breakfast. And by "better" I don't mean "healthier"; I mean that my vacation breakfasts actually represent breakfast and aren't just leftover crackers from the night before. There were all sorts of good ways to start off your day – pancakes, eggs cooked like 4o different ways, and don't even get me started on the endless amounts of bacon. You can just pocket that stuff for a snack later by the pool. It's crazy.

Every morning after you get home, it's like nobody even cares that you'd really like some French toast. You waltz into the kitchen and nada. No person saying "What can I make you?" followed quickly by "It's a pleasure." So, I end up making my own dang breakfast again and it just isn't quite as glamorous. Ladies and Gents, I'd like to introduce you to my Quaker friend. He makes oatmeal. Oh wait, I mean I make oatmeal.

- It's no longer acceptable to just go anywhere you want in your swimming suit. In tropical locals, swimwear is completely appropriate attire for any occasion. Apparently it's not part of the "dress code" in the office. Whatever that means. But do you like my corn rows?

I have issues . . . lots of them.

"Far be it for me to ever let my common sense get in the way of my stupidity. I say we press on." –
Sherrilyn Kenyon

Sometimes . . . I lie.

I have a complex. I think it may be one that a lot of people silently suffer from but since I find it not only disturbing but mildly humorous, I think this is an appropriate venue to talk about it.

I called my doctor today (how many stories start this way and you immediately want to check out?) to schedule an appointment - you know, the kind that generally only happens once every twelve months. (I could say this same sentence 15 years ago and everyone would automatically assume I was talking about my physical that I would always get before basketball camp. If it makes you feel more comfortable, we can stick to that.). Anyway, as I called today, I was notified by the appointments desk that my doctor's next available appointment is in approximately two months. Two months! Three things struck me at this very moment: first, I need to stop doing such an amazing job of telling everyone how great my doctor is because they are making it so my yearly becomes a year and a halfly. Second, I missed my calling. Apparently there is a pretty major market for doctor's that specialize in . . . ahem . . . physicals. I think I should have stuck out biology and went the way of job security.

The final thought that went through my head (and this is where the complex comes in) was (audibly): "Alright. That will give me another two months to lose more of the baby weight. Gonna get a solid C+ on this report card." Um, what? Did I just project my need for acceptance onto my doctor? Yes, yes I did.

You see, I have this issue that anytime I go and get any sort of professional service done, I, in the back of my warped head, am hoping that said professional will turn to me and say "I am not needed here. You clearly know more than I and are free to go." Or, at the very least, nod in amazement because they have never seen such a fine specimen and they feel overly privileged to be performing their service on me.

So back to the doctor; during my pregnancy, my doctor was amazing at reminding me to eat healthy and try to not gain too much weight. (Pregnant brain translation: eat all the chocolate cake you are craving. Who is going to say anything?) So, I did what any patient would do and took her advice: I ate more vegetables (with my hamburger) and drank skim milk (after those chocolate cookies). Ok, I wasn't horrible but I could have been better.

One week, my husband went to an appointment with me and over the previous two weeks, I had gained like five pounds or something that sounded WAY more astronomical to the doctor than it did to me, apparently. So, she started quizzing me about what I was eating.

"What did you have for breakfast?"
"Some eggs . . . on a piece of toast."
"Hmm . . . . ok. Maybe just egg whites next time? Lunch?"
"Some carrots and a turkey sandwich."
"Hmm . . . . what kind of bread?"
(Here was my opening)
"White. . . I probably should have done wheat (like THAT made five pounds of difference)."
"Yeah, let's try that."

When she left to get some test results, my cute husband turned and smiled at me . . . and I buckled. "Ok, I know I didn't eat toast and eggs for breakfast but if I had said that I ate a breakfast burrito the size of a toddler, she would have killed me!!"

In my head, I got away with it. Clearly I could blame all of my weight gain on the fact that I ate white bread instead of wheat. Gluten. That's a thing, right? Reality would say that my doctor walked straight into the hall and said "Eggs and toast my. . ."

If you thought that the doctor was the only place I flat out lied about how well I take care of myself, you underestimate me. I'm nothing if not consistent. Here are some other places that I find myself fibbing on a regular basis:

The Pedicure
Do I think I have the most fabulous feet in the world? No. Do I like to think that I offer some sort of relief to my pedicuring vixen that my feet are not the grossest or moldiest thing they have ever seen? Yes. The point of a pedicure: to relax, get your feet treated and PAY to walk out with perfectly manicured toes. So naturally, it only makes sense that I remove my chipped nail polish and pumice my feet for a week before I go in for said treatment, just so my non-English-speaking friend will be the "lucky" one in the salon that day. I don't want them to work too hard for my money (or talk about me when I leave . . . or while I'm sitting right there, for that matter).

The Dentist
I have straight teeth and I brush. . . but never as hard or as long as I do on the day I go to the dentist; Most of the time I even rinse and floss before I go so that when he asks if I perform said rituals, I can say "Sure do." without totally lying; never mind that one day of rinsing will not fool a seasoned professional or even a third year dental student as is usually the case in those "cheap cleaning"

mail advertisements that I respond to. The point is that in my head, it totally fools the dentist and every assistant within five miles of that drill. "What amazing teeth!" they'll say. "I've never met anyone that actually flosses every day!" they'll declare. So, I sit in that chair ready for him to say "I have never seen such a fine smile," and then proudly send me on my way. Usually though, reality sets in and for one reason or another, I can't feel the right side of my face for the next few hours. BUT I RINSED!?!?!

The Hairdresser
Did I just wash and straighten my hair before I got here? Noooo. "What? Oh my gosh, no. This awful mess? Seriously, I haven't washed it in a couple of days and it just looks so dirty right now." False. I washed. I washed twice. And I used volumizer to pump up my greasy roots. I also pulled out the couple of gray hairs in the front so that you will wonder out loud how my color holds so well. Must be that expensive shampoo that I use every day. Must be that.

I realize that I need to get this lying in check but I can't help myself. Maybe my doctor can help me through my issues when I get in to see her. That is if she can get past being so proud of me for eating healthy . . . starting the Saturday before my appointment.

Common Sense

If I had my way, we would just rename this phenomenon to "sense" or "uncommon sense" for obvious reason. The title here denotes that at least a good portion of the population have a thread running through them that would tell them "Yes, good. No, bad." But I argue that finding this little voice commonplace at all is a farce; common sense is about as "common" these days as a group of teenage boys at a Bieber concert.

In my house growing up, we had a saying (and when I say "we" I, of course, mean my dad): Use your head for something besides a hat rack. When I was much younger, like two, this really confused me because I didn't even wear hats that often. But as I came into my own, I think it was around my fourth birthday, it finally all made sense: oh, I'm actually supposed to think *before* I do/say things.

As I've gotten older, I realize that there is exactly 2% of the population that received this same advice growing up. Don't blame yourself, we'll chalk this one up to "bad parenting" so we can move on without any guilt or feel-bads.

I think in order for us to make a societal comeback of sorts from all of the parenting misses over the past decades, we should consider introducing a series of classes into the already air-tight school curriculum of our youngsters. My suggested course outline is as follows:

Introductory Course: All choices have consequences

- Part 1: You'll get further in life if you don't act like an idiot

- Part 2: Thinking before you speak

I bet you were thinking that this would warrant some hefty outline in order to cover all of the common sense mishaps that seem to prevail in and around us today; like there would be multiple courses and various parts to each. Sorry to disappoint. This covers it. My simple two-part plan basically covers the necessary lessons that so many seem to be lacking. All scientific research indicates that completion of this course will result in a 47% decrease in general stupidity.

Labeling

I'm not talking about the people kind of labeling because while I would like to get on an emotionally-charged, "this is good for humanity" soapbox where I tell you how it's wrong to judge other people, the other side of that soapbox would have a giant tag that says "A hypocrite stands here" and I'm just not ready for that kind of ridicule or commitment; if I write about not labeling people, I'd certainly have to remove it from my list of "favorite bad things to do" and I'm just not at a point where I can stop yet. So, you can stop feeling like this is going to be a section of my book plagued with guilt, right? Moving on.

I'm here to talk about literal labeling - you know those little machines that print out labels, those ones that are basically like crack by way of addiction and like Costco by way of justification. (Can't you justify buying just about anything in bulk when you go into Costco? "Well who wouldn't need a 10 year supply of hot pockets?" or "Of course mascara should only be sold in a 50 gallon drum. I can refill. . .") Once the labels start coming out, you think you have to label everything and it's a cold day in Phoenix before you can stop.

This all came to a head the other day when I was at work and noticed that the three utensil holders on the table all had labels on them, instructing the user (myself) which utensil I was about to use. Right then the question came into my mind "Which comes first - knowing what a fork is or knowing how to read the word 'fork'?" It's an age-old mystery, just like the chicken and the egg. I would assume that most people can recognize a fork before they know how to read the word. Fair assumption?

I think that in cases like this, labeling just doesn't make the least bit of sense. I can look down into the container and see what's in it just as fast as reading the front. So, I pose the question to the masses: Is this labeling necessary?

Labeling items that are, on their own, fairly apparent is ridiculous. I don't have a label on my screen that says "computer" nor is there a label on the big brown block of wood at the entrance to our office that says "door". Are we learning English? Isn't it recognizable for what it *is*?

I respect labeling solid containers that you don't want to sift through for a certain holiday decoration or winter clothes but only if the contents aren't readily available for your perusal anyway. When you start labeling clear totes or kitchen utensils, I start thinking that you were just bored and needed something to label. . . other than your neighbor (OK, you didn't really think I'd get through this entire section without a little labeling guilt/humor, did you? Oh you did? That's cute. . .)

I tell you what, these label makers are like drugs (so I hear) or chocolate (so I know). I'm actually surprised that I don't walk into more "organized" houses with the owner twitching in the corner, labels on the cupboards in the kitchen so guests can stop asking all of those annoying "where are your. . ." questions when they visit. I hope the reality TV people are reading this – I smell a new season of "Intervention" in the works. I'm here if you need some creative input or need suggestions of nut-balls that I think would be a good fit for this television fiasco.

When driving. . .

Ok, I'm not even going to pretend that I am the best driver in the world and that I haven't inadvertently made a few mistakes on the road but this is a serious pain point, people, and I think we need to talk about it.

The horn in your car was actually installed as an emergency device; otherwise, it would be more appropriately marked with a sticker that says "Press and hold when agitated." I think people use their car horns way too much – well before it's even warranted in the average highway-driving scenario. Oddly enough, the people who seem to have the greatest issue are the ones that have the worst driving habits, like somewhere in their secret "How to be a terrible driver" manual, it states "Making major traffic violations are fine as long as you quickly honk for an extended period of time and blame someone else for your actions, i.e. yell out your window and/or send off the one-finger salute." You can easily recognize these people because generally, they have at least one side mirror dangling by a thread or a 311 sticker in their back window.

If you find yourself being horn-dependent, I have a solution for you: take your car into a mechanic and have him mess with your fuses. You see, when I was 16 I had this fantastic gold car that had all of the upgrades – manual windows and manual sliding locks. (I'm nervous that people reading this may not even know what I'm talking about. Let's just say it was a daily bicep workout.) Don't get me wrong, I was thrilled to have *anything* that would drive so I'm not complaining. The best feature of my car was that the horn worked . . . once. You see, something was mis-wired in the car and I could honk the horn but only once; as soon as I would honk it, the interior light in my car would stop working and the horn would be caput until I put in a new fuse. It was a lot of work. So, knowing that, I had to really, really want to use my horn in order to make the honk worth it. Crossing your wires works like a charm, kids. It's either that or weekly yoga classes to harness your chi. The wires are cheaper than stretchy pants though and much less awkward.

In the bathroom. . .

Just when you thought there was something still sacred about the bathroom, I go and talk about it openly in my book. Gentlemen, if there are any of you still reading, don't fret; this has nothing to do with putting the seat back down. In fact, because (outside of my home) I have very little idea what happens in the men's room, this is really an etiquette outline for the ladies.

I know that whatever issues you have going on in your life are obviously pressing – things are so complicated these days. But regardless of how pressing (and I mean unless someone is physically in the process of dying), there is zero need to talk on the phone in a public restroom. Zero need. You'll note that I said nothing about your restroom at home – do whatever you want there. Why is it different? Because at home, you don't rope me, the innocent bystander, into the situation with your mindless chatter.

On more than one occasion I've been in a stall, doing what you do in restroom stalls, and have had one of these 'toilet talkers' enter the restroom. This situation is always worse at work because no matter who is on the other side of that door, you can assume that you probably know them to some degree.

So, the toilet talker walks in either mid-dial or just as the person on the other end says "hello?"

"Hey, how's it going?"

This is where I start to panic. As I mentioned, I'm in my stall, unable to see that this person is on the phone so now I'm wondering, "Are they talking to me? Are they being polite but *clearly* violating bathroom protocol by trying to talk to me over the stall?" So, even though it goes against everything I stand for, I respond:

"Hey, I'm good. How are you?"

Inevitably, my prompt reply is met with some snarky remark into the cell phone: "Hang on; someone in the bathroom is trying to talk to me."

Wait! Wait! I'm not going to get blamed for this — like I'm the one violating bathroom etiquette by talking over the stall. All I wanted was a quiet moment and you had to be all Chatty Cathy. And don't act so "annoyed" that I replied! How was I supposed to know you weren't talking to me? I can't see through these stalls! Maybe if your shoes lit up when you were on the phone, you'd have a case but they don't. Ugh, now I'm the weird one.

So, I do what any person would do: I shut my mouth and think of all of the nasty things I should say back to the creeper that is pooping while she chats and hide in my stall until she has washed up and is far enough down the hall that she won't see me exiting the bathroom.

I've never understood phones in bathrooms. Not ever. It amazes me when I go to a hotel and as a manifestation of their "class", they put a phone near the toilet. What is classy about that? Is it a sign of business prowess — knowing that on occasion a businessman might have a potty emergency in the middle of a conference call and this divine phone placement will save him the embarrassment of excusing himself in the middle of said call and he can stay on the line while he handles his other "business"? Think about it before you answer . . . is it MORE embarrassing to excuse yourself or to have a potential client hear you poop? Think hard little grasshopper.

Is the phone in there in case, while reading the daily comics, you get the urge to order room service? Isn't that an odd time to be thinking about food INTAKE? Ok, I'm dry heaving. Enough said.

I feel like maybe the bathroom isn't the place to conduct your phone business. Especially when all anyone can hear is cordiality and nonsensical banter coming from your side, I can't imagine that the person on the other end is having a philosophically-rooted conversation and all you have to say is "Totally."

One more thing . . .

My last piece of bathroom advice: always use the spray. I know that you are thinking "If the bathroom smells like "Fresh Linen" or "Jasmine Wildflower", the person after me is certainly going to know that I pooped." Well, my friends, better that they know that you *do* poop than them knowing that you do and knowing what it smells like. Always default – no matter how cool you are, the spray stinks less than your poopy.

Some Random Thoughts

You know, just in case this book wasn't chaotic enough?

You had to know that there would be more, right? I barely touched on life's most important topics! So, to pacify myself and my loyal readers that made it to this point in the journey, I've included some random tidbits that have come across my mind while writing. You're welcome.

- If you ever plan to run for office or enter a pageant: never, under any circumstances, regardless of what the creepy fella behind the lens tells you or what the contract says, never take nudy pictures. It won't end well. Ever.

- Amendment to previous point: ~~If you ever plan to run for office or enter a pageant: never, under any circumstances, regardless of what the creepy fella behind the lens tells you or what the contract says,~~ Never take nudy pictures. It won't end well. Ever.

- When posting on social media, you don't need to sign off after your message – "Love, Sue". You see the cool thing about social media is that you are already identified – generally your name, and quite possibly even your picture, accompanies any comments that you make so that little add-on at the end: not necessary. You aren't writing a letter. Middle-aged people everywhere: please read this over and over again.

- Tetris or Dr. Mario? The debate continues.

- When your brother tells you to lay down underneath a swing to see "how close" he can get to your face without actually kicking you, don't do it. It's a trap.

- When you call someone on the phone and they tell you that you have the wrong number, believe them. It just gets awkward to argue with someone who knows that their phone rang and that the person you are asking for is not there. Unless you are the police; then you should do whatever you want because you are the police.

- International standards for getting a massage vary greatly by country; particularly as it concerns how far down your back is "too far down your back" while getting massaged. Research carefully.

- Having friends is overrated . . . unless you want to go places or do things or talk to people. Then it's necessary.

- It's a really good thing that Facebook doesn't track who and how many times people look at photos. If they did, I bet there would be a dramatic increase in restraining orders . . . probably against me.

- All campsites should be equipped with flushing toilets. No, the outhouses don't count. No, they don't. No they don't. I'll push this all day – seriously I will. Don't make me.

- For those of you that feel like there was no closure . . . the relish tray debacle turned out ok. Our moms grew up in the same neighborhood and apparently cheese-in-a-can was issued in the mail the week before Thanksgiving like it was some sort of detergent sample. Both moms find it totally acceptable.

- Eating an entire bucket of anything is probably a bad idea.

- You shouldn't hit people . . . unless there is absolutely no other option. In which case you need to make sure that you do it hard enough that they either fall down or at least double over in pain so that you can make a speedy getaway.

- Believing in you is good. Believing is something outside of you is better. Believing in unicorns is just plain crazy.

Acknowledgments

I bet you wish you were nicer to me, huh? Your name could have ended up in here. Take that, third grade nemesis.

It all started on a warm spring day in 1982. . .

Ok seriously, there are so many people to thank in this section that I don't know where to begin. And I figure that I had better make it funny or you won't read this part . . . and this is the next holiday or anniversary or birthday gift for everyone included so I really need everyone to read this part to give my gift some backing. So read on, seriously.

Thank you to my dad. Thank you for making me laugh at myself before anyone else had a chance to; it saved me from some potentially awkward situations and created even more – hence all of the amazing material in this book. You make me laugh like nobody can and I hope that I get to be more and more like you as I get older (and balder?).

Thank you to my sweet momma. Nobody has the patience that you have and that can be proven by the fact that you never moved far away from me and Dad and Dall when our jokes got really bad. You are my bestest and I love you more than I can say. Thanks for believing in me, no matter what crazy ideas I come up with, and for teaching me about the kind of mom that I want to be.

Brother: you've always been my hero . . . except for those three times that we fought when we were young. Hulk Hogan was my hero then. But I got over that. I'm proud of the man that you are and grateful that I always know that you are proud of me . . . because you tell me that you are; and I need that. Thanks for believing in me so that I could believe in myself.

Thank you to my fantastic editing team, Dallas, Momma Hansen and Natalie. If I didn't trust your humor and intelligence, I would have sent this somewhere else to be edited. So I guess I'm saying you are all smart and funny. And now it's forever in print to prove it. They are, people. Smart and funny. And good looking.

To my husband Trevor: thank you for all that you put up with. Thank you for laughing at all the right times (usually when I say "Laugh; that was funny." At least you are obedient.) and for supporting me in whatever I do. I never could have imagined a life like the one we've built – you've made it more fantastic than I could have ever hoped for. No matter how many times I've heard your stories, I'm grateful every day that you are here to tell them.

Thanks to my babies for all of the good material. My life is exponentially funnier now that you are in it. It's also way more filled with love than I ever thought possible. You are the best thing I've ever done.

The people that surround me are the funniest, coolest people on the planet. I know this because I checked. Thanks for laughing with me and at me. More importantly, thanks for teaching me about grace and how to love life and showing me that doing hard things is an important part of life. (Important **side note**: If you think you might fall into this group of people, you do.)

I am blessed.

-Carlee

Made in the USA
San Bernardino, CA
10 April 2015